Dachshunds

SHEILA WEBSTER BONEHAM, PH.D

Dachshunds

Project Team
Editor: Stephanie Fornino
Copy Editor: Ellen Bingham
Interior Design: Leah Lococo Ltd. and Stephanie Krautheim
Design Layout: Stephanie Krautheim

T.F.H. Publications
President/CEO: Glen S. Axelrod
Executive Vice President: Mark E. Johnson
Publisher: Christopher T. Reggio
Production Manager: Kathy Bontz

T.F.H. Publications, Inc.
One TFH Plaza
Third and Union Avenues
Neptune City, NJ 07753

Discovery Communications, Inc. Book Development Team
Marjorie Kaplan, President and General Manager, Animal Planet Media
Patrick Gates, President, Discovery Commerce
Elizabeth Bakacs, Vice President, Creative and Merchandising
Sue Perez-Jackson, Director, Licensing
Bridget Stoyko, Designer

Printed and bound in China.
09 10 11 12 13   5 7 9 8 6 4

Library of Congress Cataloging-in-Publication Data
Boneham, Sheila Webster, 1952-
  Dachshunds / Sheila Webster Boneham.
      p. cm. – (Animal Planet pet care library)
  Includes index.
  ISBN 978-0-7938-3785-4 (alk. paper)
  1. Dachshunds. I. Animal Planet (Television network) II. Title.
  SF429.D25B66 2007
  636.753'8–dc22
                        2007006237

The Leader in Responsible Animal Care for Over 50 Years!®
www.tfh.com

Table of Contents

Chapter 1

Why I Adore My

Dachshund

Dachsie, wiener dog—whatever you call him, the Dachshund is a lot of dog in a low-slung package. At once sweet, feisty, loyal, fierce, mischievous, standoffish, tough, and vulnerable, the Dachshund has earned himself many loyal fans. Let's look at the traits that have made him one of the world's most popular companion dogs.

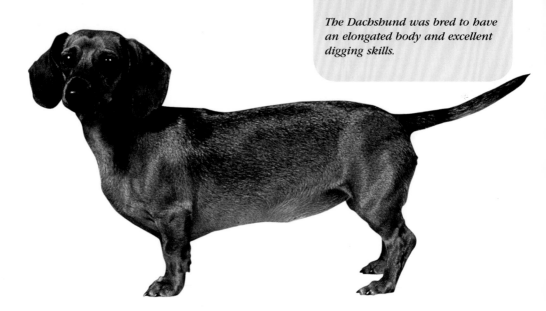

The Dachshund was bred to have an elongated body and excellent digging skills.

Form Follows Function

The Dachshund was developed in Germany during the eighteenth and nineteenth centuries by combining several breeds to produce a tough dog with an elongated body and excellent digging skills, characteristics that most modern Dachsies retain.

The modern name *Dachshund* is German for "badger dog" and shows us that the modern Dachsie's forebears were used to track badgers into their burrows and kill them or drag them out. But badgers weren't their only prey; they also hunted or trailed foxes, ermines, boars, hares and rabbits, and deer.

The closest that most modern Dachsies ever come to a badger or boar is on nature shows on television, but your dog's heritage is immediately evident in his physical traits. His short legs and strong feet are perfect for digging—you've probably already discovered this if you have moles or other underground attractions in your yard. His long, low body is like a flexible torpedo, able to speed through narrow underground passages and turn around in small spaces. These characteristics were developed through *selective breeding* over many generations, and responsible breeders strive to preserve this hunting heritage.

One Breed, Many Looks

When you think of a Dachshund, you probably imagine short legs, a long body, a long nose, and long ears. But within these general guidelines, an array of coat types, coat colors, and body sizes creates a variety of looks within this one breed.

Coat Types
Dachshunds come in three coat varieties, each with its own distinctive appearance.

The Smooth-Coated Dachshund
The best known is no doubt the smooth Dachshund, who epitomizes the classic look of the breed—sleek and elegant, the short, smooth-lying coat silky and gleaming.

The Longhaired Dachshund
The longhaired Dachshund looks rather like a short-legged setter with

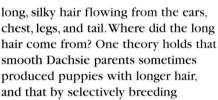

Selective Breeding
Selective breeding is a process of choosing animals with the physical and mental traits that people want and breeding them together in hopes that each generation will be a little closer to perfection.

long, silky hair flowing from the ears, chest, legs, and tail. Where did the long hair come from? One theory holds that smooth Dachsie parents sometimes produced puppies with longer hair, and that by selectively breeding these puppies together, breeders eventually were able to breed longhairs consistently. Another theory holds that smooth Dachshunds were crossed with spaniels. The softer personality of most longhairs gives some credence to this theory.

Dachshunds come in three coat varieties: longhaired (far left), wirehaired (center), and smooth coated (far right).

The Wirehaired Dachshund

The wirehaired Dachshund's whiskered face and terrier-like rough coat give him a smart, slightly comical look. Wirehairs owe their hard, protective coats to hard-coated terriers and wirehaired pinschers who were crossed with smooth Dachsies many generations ago.

Coat Colors and Patterns

Smooth and longhaired Dachsies come in many colors. One-colored dogs are either solid red or solid cream. Two-colored Dachshunds can be black, chocolate, blue, wild boar (a blend of gray and black hairs), and fawn (called "Isabella"), each with tan "points," or trim, on the face, chest, legs, and tail. Wirehaired Dachshunds also come in those colors, but in the United States, most are wild boar, black-and-tan, and various shades of red.

A number of color patterns also occur in Dachshunds, including dapple, double dapple, brindle, sable, and piebald. (See the sidebar "Coats of Many Colors" for more information.) A small bit of white on the chest is allowed but not considered desirable.

Size

One size does not fit all Dachshunds, either. The larger standard Dachshund weighs 16 to 32 pounds (7 to 14½ kg), while the miniature Dachshund weighs 11 pounds (5 kg) or less. Although not an official variety of Dachshund, some dogs fall between the standard and the mini in weight and are known fondly, if informally, as "tweenies."

Different Coats, Different Personalities

Although Dachshunds with all three types of coats share many of the same traits, owners and breeders say they also differ in some ways. The *smooth Dachshund* most closely embodies the traits of his original badger-hunting ancestors. He tends to be aloof with strangers, loyal to his family, at times intolerant of strangers and changes in his surroundings, and stubborn. The *longhaired Dachshund* is said to be more laid back and sweet, perhaps a legacy of the spaniels who also may have given him the long, silky coat. Many longhairs also love water, another sporting dog trait. Their forebears were sometimes used to hunt otters in their burrows along riverbanks. The *wirehaired Dachshund* is more terrier-like than the other two varieties—he's an outgoing clown, full of energy, and persistent in pursuit of a goal. Perhaps the coat does make the dog!

Coats of Many Colors

"Dog people" use special terms to refer to coat colors and markings. Here are the names for the rainbow of coats among Dachshunds.

Black-and-tan	A black body with tan "points" on the eyebrows, chest, and legs; around the anus; and along the underside of the tail to one-third its length.
Brindle	A pattern of black stripes over a lighter coat.
Dapple	A splotchy look caused by a gene that "dilutes" the basic coat color, creating areas of base color mingled with a lighter shade.
Double dapple	A dapple who has inherited two dapple genes, one from each parent. Double dapples often have large areas of white on their bodies. They usually have serious congenital malformations of the eye and are often deaf.
Isabella	A fawn color.
Red	A rich, warm brown.
Piebald	White patches over the main color.
Points	Tan markings on the eyebrows, shoulders, and legs; around the anus; and under the tail.
Sable	Black tips on brown hairs.
Wild boar	A blend of gray and black hairs.

Dachsie Traits and Personality

Of course, there's more to a Dachsie than his looks. Like all dogs, Dachshunds possess some personality traits and tendencies that people like and some that people don't like as much.

Adaptability

One feature that attracts a lot of people to the Dachsie is his adaptability. He can fit into an apartment if given daily walks or can live on a farm with room to run (and dig).

Barking Tendencies

Although they are not usually yappy dogs, Dachshunds do fancy themselves watchdogs. You have probably already noticed that your Dachsie has a big bark for a small dog and that he lets you know about anything that's going on around your home.

Cleanliness

Dachsies are on the low-maintenance end of the canine spectrum in terms of cleanliness. Although they shed, they don't do so excessively, and given clean living quarters, they have

Dachshunds can be loyal friends to children.

no doggy odor. On the other hand, most Dachshunds, like many dogs, love to roll around in any stinky stuff they can find—compost, dead animals, earthworms, you name it. This instinctive behavior is believed to mask the predator's odor from his prey. It also makes him unwelcome on most people's laps and furniture and is another excellent reason to keep your Dachsie on lead when out and about. If your Dachsie does perfume himself with something not to your taste, keep your sense of humor and give him a bath. It's just part of life with a dog.

Companionability

Your Dachshund's forebears may have worked outdoors, and he may enjoy getting out and about with you, but he's meant to live inside as part of the family. Banishing a dog to the backyard is cruel and unusual punishment. He is, after all, a social animal. Besides,

FAMILY-FRIENDLY TIP

Dachshunds and Kids

Dachshunds can be wonderful, loyal buddies for children in the right circumstances. But as with any dog, some cautions are in order. First, Dachsie loyalty can be taken too far. A dog who is loyal to his own children unto death may be reserved and even snappy with other children—and may bite if he misinterprets play as a threat. Second, children must be taught to treat your Dachsie gently and not to pick him up. His long back is prone to injury, and rough play or mishandling can cause serious damage or even paralysis.

loneliness and boredom inevitably lead to unwanted behaviors. Your Dachsie needs, wants, and deserves to be with you.

Digging Tendencies

It should be no surprise that Dachshunds like to dig. Outdoors and unsupervised, your Dachsie will dig up your lawn and garden in pursuit of grubs, worms, and moles, or for the sheer joy of feeling the earth move under his feet. Indoors, he'll burrow through blankets and pillows in search of dropped cookie crumbs or the perfect nest for napping.

Exercise Requirements

Like all hunting breeds, your Dachshund needs both physical and mental exercise. Boredom and lack of exercise nearly always lead to what you call misbehavior (although your Dachsie calls it fun!). It's worth the effort to find ways to use up your dog's energy and to work his mind. Fortunately, unlike his larger hound cousins, who need hours of running exercise, your Dachsie will probably be happy with two or three walks of a half hour or so each every day. Of course, he'll do more if you're willing. In fact, many Dachshunds are involved in a variety of canine activities. (See Chapter 8.)

Independence

Dachshunds are independent, brave, and even stubborn, especially when in pursuit of a goal. Of course, your Dachsie's goal may not be the same as yours, and although he's playful, he may have his own rules for the game. For instance, he may be thrilled when you pick up a ball, and his prey drive may tell him to chase what you throw until your pitching arm falls off, but he's not a natural retriever and may not see the point of actually returning the balls to you.

Dachshunds are intelligent dogs, and like most intelligent beings, they are curious. They are also problem solvers. These traits are virtues if you outthink your Dachsie and find ways to channel his intelligence and curiosity into safe, acceptable outlets. Obedience training and exercise will help. So does a sense of humor, because sooner or later your Dachsie is going to do something you didn't anticipate!

Like all hunting breeds, your Dachshund needs physical and mental exercise.

underground (or goodies hidden under sofa cushions). Their hunting instinct, or *prey drive*, is alive and well, and most Dachsies will go after "prey," ranging from backyard squirrels to bouncing tennis balls, with killer gusto.

Trainability

Training a Dachshund to do what you want can be a challenge, and it's important not to confuse intelligence with ease of training. The truth is that the two traits are independent of one another, and different breeds and individuals are endowed with different amounts of each. Although Dachshunds are intelligent dogs, they are not necessarily interested in doing what you tell them. When you think about the work they were developed to do, this makes perfect sense—your dog's working forebears couldn't depend on people to tell them what to do when tracking prey or when face-to-face with a well-armed foe deep underground. They had to think and solve problems on their own. And they passed those abilities to their descendants.

Loyalty

Dachsies are loyal to the point of often being one-person dogs. Even in a family environment, where the dog loves everyone, a Dachsie will likely have a favorite person—and he'll make his own choice, no matter whose dog you think he's supposed to be. That person will have a four-legged shadow whenever the Dachsie is around. Even a well-socialized dog who enjoys social activities will prefer the company of his special human, and no one will wonder who that lucky person is.

Prey Drive

Dachshunds have well-developed senses, including excellent noses for sniffing out animals hidden

Famous Dachshund Owners

Many famous people have been owned by Dachshunds, including actor John Wayne, hockey star Wayne Gretsky, artists Pablo Picasso and Andy Warhol, singers Madonna, Tracy Chapman, and Winona Judd, and writers Elizabeth George and E. B. White.

SENIOR DOG TIP

When Is My Dachsie a Senior?

Dachshunds generally live about 12 to 18 years if given proper care. They are considered seniors at approximately nine or ten years of age.

As one of those descendants, your Dachsie will learn quickly. It's your job to make it worth his while to learn what you want him to know and to motivate him to use that knowledge to behave as you want him to behave. Training methods that motivate your Dachsie with rewards—treats, play, toys—are the most effective way to help him develop his potential as a fine companion. (See Chapter 6.) You'll find that consistency, patience, and a sense of humor are also useful training tools.

Versatility

Your Dachsie's natural traits and instincts may not be put to use in pursuit of vermin, but they make him a versatile companion who can participate with you in a variety of activities. (See Chapter 8.) He can also be an outstanding pet if you understand that he comes with a long heritage as a hunter. You need to understand and provide outlets for the energy, intelligence, and persistence needed to pursue prey.

So there you have it—a captivating combination of sweetness and spunk, a wide range of sizes, three types of coats, and a rainbow of colors and markings, all in one handsome breed. Is it any wonder that the Dachshund is so well loved?

13

Chapter 2

The Stuff of
Everyday Life

If you're like the rest of us dog lovers, you'll buy your Dachsie all sorts of toys, beds, chewies, and other paraphernalia. Some things are just for fun; others make life easier. Most importantly, certain things keep your Dachsie safer and healthier. Let's take a look.

Set Up a Care Schedule

If more than one person helps to care for your Dachshund, you can make sure that everything gets done and nothing gets missed by posting a "duty schedule." An erasable calendar works well, particularly if you rotate duties. Include the time of day, people's names, and jobs (like feed breakfast, feed dinner, brush, take out to potty, clean up yard, walk, train, etc.), and have everyone check off jobs as they finish them. If you have children, a written schedule reinforces the fact that your Dachsie is a living creature for whom you are responsible, and it also ensures that your dog doesn't get two breakfasts and no walks.

Baby Gate

Baby gates are useful for keeping your Dachsie in certain parts of the house. They are available from most discount, hardware, and baby stores, and many pet supply catalogs offer special gates to accommodate wider door openings, permanent mounting on the doorframe, and so forth.

If you have a cat, a baby gate is a good way to block your Dachsie's access to the cat's dog-free zone, food, and litter box.

Bed

Even though your Dachsie may sleep in *your* bed, there still may be times when he needs a bed of his own. Dog beds come in a wide range of styles and prices, from thin pads to orthopedic foam and soft, loosely padded giant pillows. Individual dogs have individual preferences, so before you buy your Dachsie a bed, observe where he chooses to lie down in your home. Does he like lots of soft padding, or does he prefer just a rug on the floor? There's no point spending money on a bed he won't use. Choose a bed with a removable cover so that you can wash it, and be sure that the bed is large enough to accommodate your Dachshund's body when he's stretched out and relaxed.

If you have a puppy or young dog who likes to chew and rip things up, wait until he outgrows this phase before you buy him a bed.

Choose a dog bed that's suited to your Dachsie's individual preference.

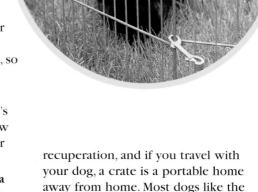

Collar

Your Dachsie needs at least one collar. If you buy only one, make it a nylon, fabric, or leather collar with a buckle or quick-release fastener. Check the fit often, and readjust or replace the collar when necessary. You should be able to insert two fingers between the collar and your dog's neck.

Collars can cause serious injuries, so for your Dachsie's safety:

- **Never leave multiple dogs alone together with collars on.** One dog's collar can trap the other dog's jaw or leg during play, injuring one or both of them.

- **Never use a slip (choke) collar on a puppy.** You can severely injure his throat and spine.

- **Never use a training collar unless you are under the supervision of a professional trainer.** Training collars can be dangerous; if the ring gets caught, the collar can seriously injure or even kill your dog.

Crate

A crate is a good investment, whether you have a puppy or an adult dog. A crate will simplify housetraining and keep your Dachsie safe and out of trouble until he can be trusted without supervision. If your Dachsie is ever ill or injured, a crate is a safe place for recuperation, and if you travel with your dog, a crate is a portable home away from home. Most dogs like the safe, cozy environment that a crate provides.

Dog crates are available from pet supply, discount, Internet, and mail-order sources. They come in many styles and prices, so choose whatever will work best for you and your dog. Select a crate that's big enough to allow your dog to stand up, turn around, and lie down comfortably. Be sure that the door fits well and latches securely so that your dog can't open it or poke his pointy muzzle or a paw through. Your Dachsie may like a nice cushion or rug in his crate, but if he chews or rips it up, leave the bedding out.

17

What About Your Long Hours Away?

If no one is home for long hours, consider having someone exercise your Dachsie during the day. This is especially important for a puppy, who can't go all day without pottying. If you hire a professional walker or pet sitter, be sure that she is insured and bonded against damages, and that she's comfortable and competent handling your dog. Check her references. You also can barter services with a reliable neighbor or friend.

Doggy day cares have become popular over the past decade. Some are well run, but be cautious. Visit the facility. It should be clean and free of hazards, with fresh water always available. All playtime should be supervised by a person with good dog skills. All dogs should be required to have current vaccinations and veterinary records, including periodic fecal exams for parasites, and your Dachsie should be protected against fleas, heartworm, and other parasites prevalent where you live. Ask how potential aggression in playgroups is managed and what response plan is in place in case of an emergency. A veterinarian should be on call, and reliable transportation should be available at all times.

Exercise Pen

If you have a puppy or an older dog who still needs supervision, or if your dog is ill or injured, you will need a way to restrict his movement. His crate is one alternative, but you may want to let him have a bit more room without giving him access to the whole house.

An exercise pen (x-pen) is an enclosure made of linked sections. Traditional x-pens are made of wire panels, but x-pens are also available in lighter-weight plastics and fabric. Many dogs learn to climb or jump out of x-pens or even lift them and crawl underneath, so never trust this enclosure to confine your dog when you aren't nearby, especially if you are not outdoors.

Food and Water Dishes

Your options for food and water dishes are practically endless. I prefer stainless steel because it's sturdy, chew proof, easy to clean, and dishwasher safe. Plastic dishes are lightweight and cheap, but they invite chewing. Also, cracks and scratches in plastic can harbor bacteria, and some dogs are allergic to plastic. Ceramic dishes are breakable, and some ceramics made outside the United States contain lead and other toxins that can leach into food and water.

Don't worry about purchasing puppy dishes—your Dachsie puppy can manage fine with an adult-sized dish.

Grooming Supplies

You'll need grooming supplies to keep

your Dachsie looking his best. The specific brushes and combs you need depend on your dog's coat type. (See Chapter 4.) You also may want a flea comb and a tick remover. (See Chapter 5.)

Doggy nail clippers are essential, and they come in two main types. The guillotine clipper has an opening into which you slip the nail, and a sharp blade that slides across the opening, cutting the nail from one side. A scissors-style clipper has two blades that cross in a scissors action, cutting the nail from both sides. An emery board made for acrylic nails is also useful for smoothing rough edges, and many serious dog fanciers use a dremel tool with a sandpaper drum to grind the nail instead of clipping. (See Chapter 4.)

Your Dachsie will need a bath

from time to time. You have lots of options, but all you really need is a mild shampoo formulated for dogs. (People shampoos will dry out your dog's skin and coat.) Avoid medicated and flea shampoos unless your vet advises you to use them.

Identification

No matter how careful you are, your Dachsie could get away sometime. If that happens, you'll want whoever finds him to know that he's your dog, so attach his current rabies and license tags, as well as an ID tag with your telephone number, to his collar. Of course, collars can be lost or removed, so a permanent form of identification as backup is a good idea.

Microchips and tattoos provide

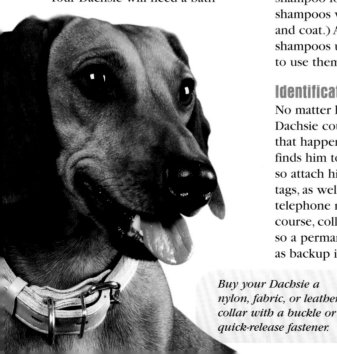

Buy your Dachsie a nylon, fabric, or leather collar with a buckle or quick-release fastener.

SENIOR DOG TIP

Helping an Older Dachsie Adjust

Most older dogs adjust quickly to new homes, but there are a few things you can do to make the transition go more smoothly for a newly adopted adult Dachsie.

- If you already have a dog, introduce the newcomer on neutral ground so that territory won't be an issue. Be ready to intervene, but let the dogs sniff one another. If they are friendly, take them home and let them continue to interact. If one or both are hostile, keep their encounters brief until they get used to one another.
- Don't leave your new Dachsie and your other dog(s) loose together when you can't supervise them for the first few weeks. Put them in different rooms, or crate one or both.
- Be cautious when introducing a new adult dog to your cat. Teach your Dachshund not to chase the cat. Create at least one dog-free zone where your cat can sleep, eat, play, and use the litter box without canine "assistance." Be sure that your cat always has an escape route, and let your cat control all interactions.
- Crate your Dachsie or confine him to one room when you can't watch him, until you're confident that he's reliable.
- Include your new dog in your regular activities as much as possible. He'll quickly adopt you as his best friend. If you already have a dog, try to give each one some private time with you every day, too.

permanent identification. A microchip is a transmitter about the size of a grain of rice encoded with a number registered to your dog. It is inserted by syringe under the skin over the shoulders. The chip can be read by a special scanner, which most shelters and many veterinarians have. Your Dachsie also can be tattooed on the belly or inside the flank with an identifying number. For more information, check with your veterinarian.

Leash

You need at least one leash, and it doesn't hurt to have one or two spares. No matter how reliable you think your

Kids and Dog Care

Owning a pet can help a child learn about love, compassion, and responsibility, but making a child completely responsible for an animal's care is unfair to both child and dog. It's also unrealistic. Children have other interests and activities, and making dog care an obstacle to those can make a child resentful. Besides, even the most dedicated child lacks the judgment and skills needed to be fully responsible for another living creature. An adult must be your Dachsie's primary caregiver.

Dachsie is, *always* leash him when outside walls or a fence. A ten-second squirrel chase into the street could end in tragedy.

A 4- to 6-foot (1.2- to 1.8-m) leather leash 1/4- to 1/2-inch (0.6- to 1.3-cm) wide is strong and relatively gentle on your hands. Many people like nylon leashes, which are cheap and come in a rainbow of colors, but some are abrasive and can burn or scrape your skin. Chain leashes are ineffective for training and can injure you

or your dog. A retractable leash is a nice way to give your dog a little more "roaming" room on walks while still keeping him safely tethered to you.

Toys and Chewies

You'll undoubtedly want to buy your Dachsie toys and safe things to chew. Be sure that they are too big for your dog to swallow, and check occasionally for loose or sharp parts. Loose stuffing, ribbons, plastic squeakers, other plastic parts, and stuffing are especially hazardous.

Good-quality chew toys cost a little more, but they are safer and last longer. Replace chew toys when they develop cracks or sharp points or edges, or when they become too small to be safe. Dogs have individual preferences, so if your Dachsie doesn't like one toy or chewie, try another kind.

Your Dachshund may not care much about material possessions (except, of course, that beat-up fuzzy toy he totes around), but having the right dog-care supplies and equipment can make life a lot easier for you. Happy shopping!

Choose toys that are too big for your Dachsie to swallow.

Chapter 3

Eating Well

What your Dachshund eats affects his health and behavior from puppyhood through old age. Many common problems can be linked to food, including dry skin and coat, itchiness, hot spots (sores), loose stools, hyperactivity, and lack of energy. A nutritious diet will go a long way toward keeping your Dachsie healthy and happy.

The number of doggy diet options is mind-boggling, and sometimes it seems that everyone has an opinion about the best way to feed a dog. Don't panic! You can ensure that your Dachshund's diet is healthful by learning some basic facts about canine nutrition and by paying attention to how your dog is doing on the food he eats. Let's begin with a look at food.

Food for Thought

Your Dachshund, like all dogs, is a carnivore—a meat eater. If he lived in the wild, he would hunt for a living. He would use his long canine teeth ("fangs") to slash and hold his prey, and his sharp, serrated molars to shear off hunks of meat. Your dog is able to digest meat proteins efficiently. Although he probably enjoys fruits and vegetables, his digestive system is unable to break down the tough cellulose walls of raw vegetable matter, so he gets few nutrients from them. Wild carnivores eat all parts of their prey and obtain some of the nutrients they need from the partially digested vegetable matter in the stomach and intestines of their prey. For domesticated carnivores, the cooked vegetables and fruits in high-quality commercial or homemade diets provide essential nutrients lacking in meats.

Your Dachshund needs carbohydrates, fats, minerals, proteins, vitamins, and water. If you feed him a high-quality dog food, he consumes these nutrients in the right amounts and should need no nutritional supplements. In fact, supplementing your dog's diet with vitamins or

A nutritious diet will go a long way toward keeping your Dachsie happy and healthy.

Common Ingredients in Commercial Dog Foods

Alpha Tocopherol: vitamin E, a natural preservative

Animal Fat: fat obtained from the tissue of mammals and/or poultry in the commercial process of rendering or extracting

Beef Tallow: fat from beef

Brewer's Rice: small bits of rice kernels broken off from larger kernels of milled rice

Brewer's Yeast: dried, nonfermentive by-product of brewing of beer and ale

Brown Rice: unpolished rice left after kernels have been removed

Chicken: flesh and skin, with or without bone, without feathers, heads, feet, or entrails

Chicken By-Product Meal: ground, rendered, clean parts of poultry, including necks, feet, undeveloped eggs, and intestines

Chicken Fat: fat from tissue of chicken

Chicken Meal: dry, ground clean combination of chicken flesh and skin with or without bones

Dehydrated Chicken: dried fresh chicken flesh (without skin, bones, feathers, heads, feet, or entrails)

Dried Beet Pulp: residue after sugar is removed from sugar beets (used as filler)

Fish Meal: dried ground tissue of undecomposed whole fish or fish cuttings, which may or may not have oil removed

Meat: flesh of slaughtered animals, including muscle, tongue, diaphragm, heart, esophagus, overlying fat, skin, sinew, nerves, and blood vessels

Meat By-Products: clean nonmeat parts of slaughtered animals, including lungs, spleen, kidneys, brain, liver, blood, bone, stomach, and intestines (does not include hair, horns, teeth, or hooves)

Poultry By-Products: nonmeat parts of slaughtered poultry, such as heads, feet, and internal organs (does not include feathers)

minerals can cause serious health problems and damage bones and tissues, especially in growing puppies.

Carbohydrates

Carbohydrates, found mostly in plants, provide energy. Corn, soybeans, wheat, and rice are common sources of this nutrient in commercial dog foods. Because some dogs are allergic to one or more of these common grains, foods are also available that offer alternative sources of carbohydrates, such as potatoes.

Fats

Meats, milk, butter, and vegetable oils are rich sources of essential fats, which insulate your Dachshund against cold temperatures, help to cushion his internal organs, provide energy, and help to carry vitamins and other nutrients through the bloodstream to his organs. Although fats are necessary in your dog's diet, they shouldn't be excessive.

Minerals

Minerals build strong bones, strengthen cell tissue, and help organs function properly. If your dog eats a high-quality diet, he's unlikely to suffer a mineral deficiency.

Proteins

Proteins are made of amino acids found in meat products and plants. Meat, fish, poultry, milk, cheese, yogurt, fish meal, and eggs are the best sources of complete proteins.

Vitamins

Vitamins are chemical compounds that support good health in several ways. High-quality dog foods provide vitamins in the proper amounts, and fruits and the livers of most animals are also rich sources of vitamins.

Water

Water is critical for life and good health. Like other animals, your dog must maintain a balance between water in and water out. He gets much of his water by drinking, but he also uses metabolic water, or water released from food as it is digested. Your dog should have access to clean, cool water at all times.

Commercial Dog Foods

You can hardly pick up a magazine or watch a half hour of television without seeing an ad for one of the many dog foods on the market—and they all claim to be the best. But not all dog foods are created equal. In fact, they range from not much better than sawdust to complete, safe, and highly nutritious.

What makes one food a higher quality than another? Ingredients! Bargain-basement foods are no bargain. They contain poorer-quality ingredients, fewer meat proteins, and more fat and fillers. A dog on such a high-fat diet may seem to be getting proper nutrition for a while, because fat provides energy. Unfortunately, the lack of protein, vitamins, and minerals in these cheap foods will lead to chronic malnutrition and the health and behavior problems that it causes, including cancers, allergies, hyperactivity, lethargy, and damage to various organs.

Higher-quality dog foods use higher-quality ingredients. Good dog foods contain few, if any, fillers, chemicals, or dyes. Your dog will digest a high-quality food more efficiently and use more of the nutrients, making for less intestinal gas and smaller stools. Higher-quality foods cost more than lesser-quality foods, but the most expensive isn't always the best. Those beautiful commercials and advertisements that some companies put out cost a lot of money, and of course the consumer pays the bill. So shop around in a pet supply store. Read the labels and make an informed choice. Some less-well-known brands have higher-quality ingredients and cost less than some of the well-known highly advertised "premium" foods.

Another consideration when comparing prices is the cost per feeding as opposed to the cost per pound (kg). When the ingredients are more nutritious, your Dachsie needs smaller amounts per meal. Feeding a poor-quality food just to save money really is foolish, because whatever you save on dog food, you'll probably pay to your vet to treat health problems caused by poor nutrition or questionable ingredients. And your Dachsie will pay, too, in a lower quality of life.

Commercial dog foods come in three common forms: dry, semi-moist, and canned.

Dry Food

Dry food, or kibble, is the least expensive (assuming equal quality) and offers several advantages. It needs no refrigeration, although it should be stored in an air-tight container, protected from heat and light, and used by its expiration date. Dogs who eat dry food usually have cleaner teeth because the dry bits scrape tartar away during chewing, and the food doesn't stick to the teeth. They also have firmer, smaller stools.

Semi-Moist Food

Semi-moist dog foods are soft chunks,

Nutritional Supplements

If your dog eats a high-quality diet, he probably doesn't need any supplements and may even be hurt by some of them. Too much calcium, for instance, can cause serious, permanent damage to growing bones in puppies and may contribute to kidney stones and other problems in adult dogs. Similarly, some vitamins, especially A and D, are toxic in large amounts. Hypervitaminosis (an excess of vitamins) is common in dogs who get supplements.

usually packaged in serving-size packets. They are more expensive than kibble and produce larger, softer stools. The soft, moist food tends to stick to teeth and harbor bacteria that cause gum disease and tooth decay. Most semi-moist foods also contain dyes and chemical preservatives that your dog just doesn't need.

Canned Food

Canned, or wet, foods are the most expensive—water increases their weight, making shipping more costly, and you also pay for the cans. They are useful for dogs with certain medical conditions, but a diet of canned food alone can contribute to a variety of problems, including flatulence, bad breath, tartar buildup and gum disease, and large, soft, smelly stools. Dishes must be washed after each canned food meal to prevent spoilage and avoid attracting insects, and open cans must be refrigerated.

Dogs who eat dry food, or kibble, usually have cleaner teeth because the dry bits scrape away tartar.

Special-Formula Food

Special-formula dog foods are available for puppies, seniors, small dogs, big dogs, active dogs, fat dogs, and even dogs of specific breeds. Whether they offer any special benefits is debatable in most cases. For example, there is no scientific evidence that senior formulas improve the health or longevity of aging dogs. Similarly, few dogs require the extra calories and protein found in "active" foods, and most good breeders and veterinarians prefer to feed puppies a high-quality maintenance food rather than a higher-calorie "puppy formula." Still, some special foods do benefit certain dogs. For example, if your Dachsie has a food-related allergy, a corn- and wheat-free food or one that uses an alternate source of meat protein (such as duck, fish, or venison) may be a good alternative.

Noncommercial Diets

Preparing a proper homemade diet can be fun, but it's also challenging. Your Dachsie doesn't need a completely balanced diet every day, but he does need to consume the proper balance of protein, carbohydrates, fats, essential fatty acids, minerals, and vitamins over the course of every few days. A proper balance of nutrients is especially important for a growing puppy—poor nutrition during the first year can cause permanent damage to the skeletal system and organs.

A complete discussion of nutritious homemade diets is beyond the scope of this book, but a number of books and websites offer accurate information on the subject. Be cautious, though—there's also a lot of bad advice out there. Don't rely on a single source, and check the writers' credentials in canine nutrition.

Home-Cooked Diet

If you like to shop and cook, and want to control the ingredients in your dog's diet, you might want to feed him a home-cooked diet that you prepare from fresh ingredients in your own kitchen. Table scraps are not a good doggy diet, but a carefully planned and prepared regime of high-quality cooked meats, eggs, cooked vegetables, dairy products, and possibly grains can give your dog all he needs nutritionally with some variety to boot.

Raw Diet

Some people believe that dogs should eat a "raw" diet of uncooked meats and unprocessed fruits and vegetables. A well-balanced raw diet provides proper nutrition and prevents some of the problems, such as common allergies, associated with some ingredients in poor-quality commercial dog foods. However, this approach to canine nutrition does pose some challenges. A variety of foods is necessary to ensure that your dog gets all the necessary nutrients in the proper proportions. In addition, you need time to prepare raw meals and proper storage for the ingredients.

This type of diet focuses on raw chicken and turkey bones, with organ meat (liver, kidney, heart, brain,

FAMILY-FRIENDLY TIP
Kids Feeding Dogs

A responsible adult should oversee your Dachshund's feeding, but kids can help. Here are some ways to make the process safe and sensible:

- Be in a position to intervene, as dogs sometimes think that they outrank children, especially young ones.
- Train your Dachsie to sit and wait politely until the child puts the food down.
- Teach your child never to tease dogs, especially with food.
- Teach your child to offer dog treats from an open palm.
- Teach your dog to allow people to take anything away from him, including food.
- Teach your children not to take food away from your dog.
- Supervise the feeding schedule and the amount of food served because a child may overfeed the dog or forget to feed him some meals.
- Don't put your dog's care in a child's hands. Pets help children learn to be responsible, but excess pressure about dog-care duties can make a child resent the dog. And it's not fair to let your dog go hungry, unexercised, unbrushed, or uncuddled if your child forgets.

Eating Well

A special-formula diet can benefit a dog who is suffering from food allergies.

tongue, and tripe) and eggs from time to time. Green leafy vegetables, which must be run though a food processor or juicer first, are often added, as well as vegetable oils, brewer's yeast, kelp, apple cider vinegar, fresh and dried fruits, and/or raw honey. Small helpings of grains and dairy products, especially raw goat milk, cottage cheese, and plain yogurt, are sometimes added.

Raw meat and poultry must be handled carefully, because they contain bacteria that can cause food poisoning. Raw meats also can harbor parasites that can be passed to your dog or to human members of your family, so it's essential to keep all utensils and work spaces scrupulously clean and to wash your hands with soap and water after handling raw meat.

Feeding Schedules

If you ask your Dachshund when he should eat, he'll probably say "Right now!" But because you are in charge of his meals, it's your job to feed him on a schedule that fits into your own while also promoting his health and well-being. Let's look at the options.

Free Feeding

Is it true that dogs who have access to food all the time won't get fat? No! In fact, free feeding—perpetual access to food—often results in canine obesity and/or picky eating habits. If you travel with your dog, free feeding is impractical, and if you board him when you're away, he'll be fed on schedule, adding more stress to the experience. Also, if your Dachsie has any issues with dominance, resource guarding, or aggression, having control over his own food can make the problem worse.

Scheduled Feeding

Feeding your Dachsie on a regular schedule gives you better control over his food intake and therefore his weight. Because lack of appetite is often the first sign of illness, scheduled feedings make it easier to monitor your dog's health. Also, achieving and maintaining housetraining is easier because regular meals make for regular elimination. If you use treats to motivate and reward your dog in training, he'll be more interested in them if he can't eat whenever he wants. And having control of his food clearly makes you your dog's leader.

Clean, fresh water, on the other

hand, always should be available to your dog except in special situations. If you are housetraining a puppy, you should limit water before bedtime. If your Dachsie will be undergoing certain veterinary procedures, you will have to withhold water for a certain period. Otherwise, water is essential for your dog's health.

Feeding Guidelines

Although there is no single "correct" approach to feeding, some general guidelines do apply to feeding dogs at different stages in their lives. The number of meals and times you feed your dog will depend in part on your schedule and in part on your Dachsie's age.

Puppies

Young puppies need to eat more frequently than older puppies and adults because their stomachs are too small to hold all the food they need in two servings. Most breeders recommend three or four meals a day for a Dachshund puppy who is 7 to 16 weeks old. Younger puppies may need to eat more frequently—four or five times a day. Take the advice of your breeder or veterinarian. Meals should be spaced as evenly as practical. Allow at least a couple of hours between the last meal and bedtime so that your pup potties before bedtime.

While your Dachsie is growing, monitor his growth and condition closely. A healthy puppy is neither skinny nor fat. He should show good bone and muscle development and a

Feed Treats Wisely

Too many treats can turn your Dachsie into a blimp or a beggar. To keep treats under control, follow these guidelines:

- Remember that food does not equal love. You can express your feelings for your Dachsie just as well with a belly rub, ear scratch, game of fetch, or walk around the block.
- Use treats to reward your Dachsie but not just for breathing. Have him do something, like perform an obedience command, to earn a reward.
- Remember that treats affect the nutritional balance and total calories of your Dachsie's diet.

nice shiny coat, as well as be active and alert. As your Dachsie matures, he'll need fewer calories per day, even if he's active.

Adults

Adult Dachsies should eat two or three times a day. Dachshunds are susceptible to a life-threatening problem called *bloat* (see Chapter 5), and dogs who eat just once a day are at a much higher risk.

Seniors

The best way to feed a senior canine is a topic of considerable debate. If your older Dachsie is healthy and in good condition, he doesn't need any change in his diet. Some elderly dogs do have trouble digesting their food efficiently and can suffer from malnutrition even when eating a high-quality diet. If your senior Dachshund is losing weight, talk to your vet. Your dog may benefit from a food with higher caloric density.

Senior dogs sometimes lose interest in their food as their senses become less sharp. If your older Dachsie is healthy but indifferent about his food, try warming it to make it more fragrant. A little warm water or unsalted broth over dry kibble works well, as does a few seconds in a microwave for soft foods. (Be careful not to serve the food too hot!) Or try adding a spoonful of cottage cheese, plain yogurt, or high-quality canned dog food—but watch the calories. Some elderly dogs also do better with more frequent, smaller meals, and I have had several who didn't want to eat early in the morning but gobbled their breakfasts at noon.

If your Dachsie stops eating for more than a day—less if he has a chronic health problem or other obvious symptoms—consult your vet. Lack of appetite or an unexplained weight change can indicate a serious problem. Dogs with chronic problems also may suffer from dehydration.

If your senior Dachsie has trouble getting around, ensure that he has easy access to water, and if necessary, add water to his food.

Slim and Trim, or Canine Football?

Although a short little dog so fat that his belly drags on the ground may seem funny at first glance, obesity is no laughing matter. Excess weight carries health hazards, and that's as true for dogs as it is for people. Food makes dogs happy, so most people give their dogs too much of it. All too often, the result is an obese pet.

For the Dachshund, especially, excess weight adds to the ever-present risk of back problems. (See Chapter 5.) Other serious weight-related health problems include heart disease, diabetes, pancreatitis, respiratory problems, orthopedic problems, and arthritis. If your Dachsie is fat, he will overheat and tire more quickly. His

Adult Dachshunds should eat two or three times a day.

Dachshund Feeding Chart

Age	Puppies (7 weeks to 4–6 months)	Adolescents (4–6 months to 18–24 months)	Active Adults (2–7+ years)	Sedentary Adults (2–7+ years)	Seniors (7 years and older)
Times per Day	3 or 4	2–3	2	2	2–4
Best Food	Adult maintenance diet, or puppy formula until 4–6 months	Adult maintenance diet	Adult maintenance diet	Adult maintenance diet in moderation; low-calorie adult food in some cases	Adult maintenance diet; senior formula if desired

life won't be as much fun as it should be, and he will probably die younger than he would if you kept the weight off of him.

Ideally, your Dachsie will tip the scales at his proper weight from puppyhood through old age, but extra weight can sneak on before you realize it. Unfortunately, many vets see so many fat dogs that they don't always alert their clients to early signs of excess weight. However, you can learn to use your hands and your eyes to determine whether your dog is healthy. Also, weigh him at regular intervals so that you know whether he's gaining or losing weight.

Keep your Dachshund at a healthy weight by feeding him right and by giving him enough exercise.

Is Your Dachshund Overweight?

To check for pudginess, place your thumb on one side of your Dachsie's spine and your index finger on the other. Start at his shoulders and move your fingers along his spine toward his tail. You should easily feel the ribs that are attached to the vertebrae. Next, look down on your dog's back when he's standing. He should have a distinct "waist" where his body narrows between his ribs and his hips. If you can't feel ribs or see a waist, your Dachshund is too fat.

How to Take Off the Excess Weight

Don't panic—it is possible to take weight off a pudgy pooch. Here are some tips for doggy dieters:

- The recommended servings on commercial dog food containers are much more than the average dog needs. Use them only as rough starting points. If your dog is fat, he needs fewer calories, no matter what the bag says.

- Measure your dog's food with a standard measuring utensil to be sure that he's getting what you think he's getting.

- To take weight off your dog, you must reduce his caloric intake. Most dogs plead starvation even when they get plenty of food, and most will eat whatever is available. For a wild canine who never knows when he'll get his next meal, it makes good survival sense to eat as much as possible when food is

SENIOR DOG TIP

Feeding the Senior Dachsie

If your senior Dachshund is healthy and in good condition, he probably doesn't need any change in his diet just because of his age. There is no scientific evidence that so-called "senior" dog foods offer most older dogs any more benefits than a high-quality adult or maintenance food. However, some elderly dogs have trouble digesting their food efficiently and can suffer from malnutrition even when eating a high-quality food. If your old Dachsie loses weight or shows other signs of insufficient diet, talk to your vet. Your dog may benefit from a food with higher caloric density. Some elderly dogs also do better when their daily ration is split into three or four meals throughout the day.

available. But for your pet dog, the next meal is no problem. Eating too much is the problem, and you are responsible for seeing that your Dachshund doesn't succumb to his ancestral appetite.

- If you really think that your dieting Dachsie is still hungry, you can add bulk without calories to make him feel more full. One way is to measure a meal's worth of kibble, divide it in two, and soak one half in water for a half hour or so. The pieces will absorb water and expand. At mealtime, mix the dry portion with the soaked portion and serve. Or add a high-fiber, low-calorie food to your dog's dry food—good choices are unsalted green beans (uncooked fresh beans or frozen beans are fine; if you use canned beans, rinse them well to remove salt); lettuce or spinach; canned pumpkin (not pie filling, just pumpkin); or unsalted, air-popped popcorn (unless your Dachsie is allergic to corn).

- You might consider a weight-loss or lower-calorie food, but be careful—lots of fat dogs stay fat on long-term diets of "light" food. Most dogs do better with smaller quantities of maintenance food and more exercise.
- Treats add calories, so limit the number that you feed your Dachsie, and be sure that other members of your household don't give him extras. Or set aside part of your dog's daily food to use as treats. Most dogs think that a single piece of plain old dog food is special.

Age, exercise, general health, and other factors all affect dietary requirements. Adjust your Dachsie's food intake as his nutritional needs change. He'll live a longer, healthier, happier life and look a lot better, too.

Your Dachsie doesn't need fancy cuisine, but he does need high-quality nutrients in the right amounts. You can ensure that your dog's diet is right for him by knowing what's in his food and by learning to assess his weight and physical condition. Your reward for a little effort will be a healthier, longer-lived Dachshund.

Don't Overfeed Your Dachsie!

The Dachshund loves to eat, and yours will train you to feed him if he can. Food makes dogs so happy that it's hard to say no, but please don't turn your Dachsie into an overstuffed wiener. Excess weight is a health hazard for all dogs, but for the long-backed Dachshund, it's almost certain to lead to slipped or ruptured (herniated) spinal disks. Although some treatments are effective, damaged disks can and often do lead to pain and lack of mobility, including partial or complete paralysis. Even lean Dachsies are susceptible to disk problems (see Chapter 5), so why add to the risk?

Chapter 4

Looking Good

Your Dachshund needs to be groomed to look and feel his best. Grooming sessions shouldn't be a chore but rather special times that you spend interacting quietly with your dog. They are also an opportunity to check your Dachsie for bumps, cuts, sore spots, fleas and ticks, and other signs of trouble. Let's gather our grooming equipment and get started!

Grooming for Good Health

Regular grooming sessions are the perfect opportunity to check your Dachsie for early signs of medical problems. Be alert for:

- bumps, cuts, sores, or sensitive areas
- cuts, lumps, bleeding, or a bad odor in your dog's mouth
- excessive discharge, redness, bad odor, or tenderness in or around your dog's ears
- irritation in or around your dog's eyes
- signs of parasites or other skin problems

Grooming Supplies

Just a few basic grooming supplies will keep your Dachshund looking good.

Smooth-Coated Dachshund

- rubber curry or grooming mitt
- chamois (optional)

Longhaired Dachshund

- slicker brush
- steel comb
- spray bottle
- conditioner (optional)
- thinning sheers (optional)
- stripping knife (optional)

Wirehaired Dachshund

- straight-toothed slicker brush
- stripping knife (optional)
- scissors (optional)
- electric clipper (optional)

All Varieties

- doggy toothpaste and toothbrush
- ear cleaner
- file or dremel tool for smoothing nails (optional)
- flea comb
- nail trimmers
- shampoo formulated for dogs

Coat and Skin Care

Dachshunds are generally clean dogs who shed moderately, produce little dander, and have little doggy odor. Because they are so low to the ground, though, they tend to pick

38

Have your supplies ready before you begin to groom your Dachshund.

Regular brushing will help to keep your Dachsie's coat clean and glowing.

up debris in their travels, and like most dogs with a hunting heritage, most Dachsies will roll in stinky things to "perfume" themselves.

Brushing

Regular brushing will help to keep your Dachsie's coat clean and glowing. Brushing also stimulates circulation, keeps skin in good condition, and removes loose hair. The equipment and routine are slightly different for each of the three coat types.

How to Brush Your Smooth Coat

The smooth-coated Dachsie is a snap to groom. Simply rub the coat gently with a rubber curry (a rubber oval with a nubby surface) or a grooming mitt (a mitten with nubs in the palm) to remove dirt, stimulate circulation, and distribute skin oils through the coat. If you want make your Dachsie even glossier, finish by rubbing him with a chamois cloth. Although a daily rubdown is desirable, once a week will keep him looking good.

How to Brush Your Longhair

The longhaired Dachshund's coat requires a bit more care, but the results are worth the effort. The long, silky hair should be brushed thoroughly at least twice a week. Before you brush, spritz your dog's coat lightly with water or a diluted conditioner (1 tablespoon [14.8 ml] conditioner in 16 ounces [236.6 ml] of water) to reduce static and prevent breakage. A slicker brush, which has curved metal pins set into a flat or curved backing, works well on the longhair's coat.

The furnishings, or long hair on your longhaired Dachsie's ears,

The wirehaired Dachshund needs regular brushing to prevent tangles, stimulate circulation, and distribute skin oils through his coat.

legs, and fanny, will form mats if not brushed regularly. Work the slicker slowly through small sections of hair in the direction of growth, then smooth the sections together. After you brush your Dachsie thoroughly, go over him again with a steel comb to find any snarls or mats you may have missed. Be gentle—don't yank on tangles, and don't scrape the skin with those sharp slicker brush pins. Grooming sessions should be enjoyable.

To really look good, longhairs occasionally need to have their coats hand stripped to remove dead and straggly hairs, and their furnishings tidied with thinning shears. You can learn these skills, or you can take your longhaired Dachsie to a professional groomer every couple of months.

How to Brush Your Wirehair

If you have a wirehaired Dachsie, you probably know by now that keeping

the stylish look you see in books and shows requires some effort. Like his smooth and longhaired cousins, the wirehaired Dachsie needs regular brushing to prevent tangles, stimulate circulation, and distribute skin oils through the coat. In addition, the wirehair coat needs special attention every two to three months.

To maintain the wirehair coat's correct harsh, weather-resistant, protective texture, it must be hand stripped with a stripping knife. Although not really difficult, hand stripping does require some skill, so if you want to maintain a stripped coat yourself, offer to pay a groomer, breeder, or show handler to teach you the technique. If you don't care about keeping the coat texture, you can have your groomer give your Dachsie a pet trim with clippers. Whether he is stripped or clipped, your wirehair needs to have his beard and eyebrows trimmed and shaped every so often to keep that distinctive wirehair look.

Bathing

Dachsies normally don't need baths often, but every few months—or when he rolls in something—you'll want to bathe your dog. Although it may not be your Dachsie's favorite activity, a bath doesn't have to be a battle, either.

To accustom your Dachsie to the bathing process, teach him that the sink or tub isn't a bad place. This may take a little time and planning but will result in a dog who accepts baths without fear and resistance. To begin, put your Dachsie into the sink or tub, praise him, give him a treat, and if he's calm, lift him out. If he struggles, hold him firmly but gently in the sink and talk to him quietly. When he stops struggling, give him a treat and lift him out. Don't reward him after he gets out—you want him to understand that being in the sink, not getting out, is good. Do this once or twice a day until your dog is comfortable in the dry sink, then add a little lukewarm water. When he's comfortable getting his feet wet, begin to wet his body with lukewarm water from a sprayer or by pouring water onto him from an unbreakable container. Reward and praise him while you wet him. When he accepts that calmly, he's ready for a bath.

You can't leave your wet, soapy dog while you go get something, so have these supplies ready before you begin:

- cotton balls
- hose attachment or unbreakable container for rinsing
- mild shampoo formulated for dogs
- nonslip mat
- one or two towels
- ophthalmic ointment (optional)

How to Bathe Your Dachshund

First, brush your Dachsie to remove loose hair, tangles, and foreign matter. Insert a cotton ball gently into the

41

Grooming Table

You can groom your Dachsie on the floor or on your lap, or you can groom him on a table. Once they get used to the idea, many dogs stand still better on a table, making the job easier for both of you. Portable grooming tables are available from most pet supply stores, or you can improvise. For your Dachsie's safety:

- Use a sturdy table and be sure folding legs are locked.
- Provide a nonslip surface for your dog to stand on.
- Tie your dog or have someone hold him if you can't rely on him to stay.
- *Never* leave your dog on a grooming table unsupervised—he could be seriously injured or killed if he jumps or falls off.

opening of each ear to protect the ear canal from water. Soap can burn your dog's eyes, so apply an ophthalmic ointment (available from your vet, groomer, or pet supply store) to the eyes, or be careful not to get soap into them.

Wet your Dachsie with lukewarm water. Apply shampoo, beginning at his neck and working toward the tail, including his belly, under his back legs, and under his tail. Use a washcloth on his face to keep shampoo out of his eyes. If you dilute the shampoo (one part shampoo to one or two parts water), lathering and rinsing will be easier, and you'll save money to boot.

The Expert Knows

Make Grooming Sessions Special

You and your Dachsie should look forward to grooming sessions, not dread them. Be gentle and talk to your dog as you groom him so that he learns to trust your hands and enjoy the way they feel on his body. Reward good behavior with a small treat, a tummy rub, or a nice ear or head massage.

Nail trimming is essential to the health of your dog's feet and legs.

If your Dachsie has fleas, create a "collar" of lather high on his neck to keep them from hiding in his ears, then lather the rest of his body. Leave the lather on for about ten minutes to drown the fleas, then rinse. Regular dog shampoo works fine for this. While you're waiting, check your dog's ears and head for fleas, and remove them by hand or with a flea comb and drop them into a container of soapy water.

Rinse your dog completely—soap residue can irritate his skin. Then gently squeeze the excess water from his coat with your hands. Pat him all over with a towel. Keep him warm and out of drafts until he's completely dry. You can dry him with a hair dryer set on low or let him air-dry.

Nail Care

Most Dachshunds hate having their nails trimmed. But no matter how much your little darling protests, nail trimming is essential to the health of his feet and legs. Overgrown nails can permanently distort your dog's foot, making walking painful. If you hear your Dachsie's nails clicking when he walks, it's time for a trim.

Two kinds of nail clippers are available: the guillotine and the scissors. Whichever kind you use, keep the blades sharp and properly aligned so that they cut cleanly without pinching. An emery board made for acrylic nails is good for smoothing rough edges on tough canine nails. As an alternative to clipping, you can use a dremel tool with a sandpaper drum to grind the nail. If you want to try it,

FAMILY-FRIENDLY TIP

Kids and Dog Grooming

Your child can learn a lot about the importance of personal hygiene and responsible pet care by helping with your Dachsie's grooming. Which grooming tasks a child can undertake will depend on her age and ability; brushing is a good place to start, and kids can help with baths. More delicate tasks, such as ear cleaning, tooth brushing, and nail trimming, should be left to an adult or to an older child under adult supervision. In fact, an adult needs to supervise all grooming to be sure that the process is gentle and thorough.

pay a groomer to show you how to do it properly to avoid injury.

You'll probably never convince your Dachsie that pedicures are fun, but you can do a few things to help him accept the inevitable more calmly. When you are relaxing and cuddling, handle his feet, gently massaging and flexing his toes so that he learns that having his feet handled is not unpleasant.

How to Care for Your Dachshund's Nails

Dachshunds have dark nails, which

makes trimming more challenging because you cannot see the quick (the living portion of the nail). Also, keep in mind that your Dachsie's long back makes it difficult for him to stand on three legs for any length of time. If you do his nails with him standing, try folding the foot up toward the rear, as a farrier does when shoeing a horse, rather than pulling it forward. Your dog might be more comfortable sitting or lying down. Also, make sure that you have good light.

Use grooming time as an opportunity to check your dog for early signs of medical problems.

To trim your Dachsie's nails, hold the paw firmly but gently, and press the bottom of the foot pad lightly to extend the nail. Trim just the tip, below the spot where the nail narrows and curves downward. After you clip, check the end of the nail. A black dot near the center indicates the quick, and you've trimmed enough. All your dog's nails, front and back, need to be kept trimmed, including the dewclaws, those little nails on the insides of the legs.

If your dog struggles during this process, trim just one nail, give him a treat, and then release his paw. Handle his other paws one at a time, without clipping, then quit for a while. As he becomes more accepting, move up

to one paw at a time, and continue to play with his feet between trimming sessions. If he'll let you, progress to two paws per session, then three, then all four.

If you accidentally cut into the quick, the nail may bleed. Cornstarch or styptic powder will stop the bleeding—just put a little in a shallow dish or the palm of your hand and dip the nail into it. Reassure your dog, and give him a special treat for putting up with you.

Some Dachsies never cooperate completely, in which case you may need a helper. For some owners, regular trips to a groomer or the vet for nail trimming are well worth the cost.

Ear Care

Your Dachsie's beautiful, long, hound-style ear leathers (or flaps) are lovely, but unfortunately, they hold moisture in the ear canals, creating ideal breeding

grounds for yeast or bacteria that cause inflammation and infection. Ear mites, small arthropods related to spiders and ticks, are more of a problem for cats than for dogs, but if your Dachsie is allergic to mite saliva, even a few of the little devils will make his ears itch like mad. Plant matter, dirt, or other things also can get caught in your dog's ears and irritate or injure them. And if your Dachsie's ears itch or bother him, he may injure himself by overzealous scratching.

How to Care for Your Dachsie's Ears

Check your Dachsie's ears at least once a week during grooming time. The skin lining his ears should be clean and pink or flesh colored, not dirty, red, or inflamed. A little wax is normal, but a lot of dirty-looking gunk is not. Strong or objectionable odors are not normal either.

If you see or smell anything that doesn't look right, or if your Dachsie scratches or rubs his ears, shakes or tilts his head, or objects to having his ears handled, see your veterinarian. Ear infections are painful and can lead to permanent hearing loss. Don't try to treat an ear problem with over-the-counter or home remedies—the wrong treatment can prolong the problem and cause more damage.

If your Dachsie's ears look normal, clean them with a commercial ear cleaner or a 50-50 mixture of water and rubbing alcohol. If his ears seem very waxy or if he plays in water frequently, clean them once a week with a cleaner designed to keep the ear

canal free of excess moisture, yeast, and bacteria. (Ask your vet or groomer for recommendations.)

Ear cleaning can be messy, so do it where flying cleaner and wax won't be a problem. Squirt the cleaner into the ear, then cover the ear opening with the ear flap and massage for a few seconds. Then stand back while your dog shakes to clear his ears. When he's finished, wipe them gently with a cotton ball or tissue. Never insert anything into the ear canal—you can impact any wax that's present and injure delicate organs.

Eye Care

Your Dachshund's eyes are vulnerable to injury or irritation, just like your own, and because his eyes are much closer to the ground than yours, they are exposed to plenty of dust and debris. A few minutes a day for eye

care will prevent many problems and catch most others before they become serious.

How to Care for Your Dachshund's Eyes

Routine eye care is simple. First, protect your dog's eyes when necessary. Soap and chemicals can injure delicate eye tissues, so be careful when using shampoo, insect repellents, or other chemicals. Don't let your Dachsie hang his head out of the car window, because a fast-flying bug or bit of dirt can cause serious, permanent damage.

A little mucus at the inner corners of the eyes is normal, but built-up "eye gunk" harbors bacteria that cause infections. Gently wipe mucus away with a moist washcloth, cotton ball, or tissue once or twice a day. Redness, swelling, excess mucus or tearing, or squinting may indicate an eye infection, abrasion, or other problem. If you see any of these symptoms, call your vet immediately.

As your Dachsie ages, his eyes may become cloudy from a condition known as nuclear sclerosis, which usually does not affect vision. However, cloudiness also may be caused by a cataract, which can impair vision or even cause blindness. (See Chapter 5.) If you see changes in your Dachsie's

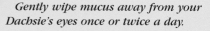

Gently wipe mucus away from your Dachsie's eyes once or twice a day.

Bad Dachsie Odors

A healthy Dachshund does not have an unpleasant odor. If your Dachsie is smelly, follow your nose, see your vet, and fix the problem. Here are some common causes of unpleasant doggy odors:

- broken or decayed teeth, or gum disease
- ear infection
- infected or impacted anal glands
- intestinal or stomach gas
- oil, bacteria, yeast, or a foreign substance on the skin or coat

eyes, ask your regular vet to have a look, or take your dog to a veterinary ophthalmologist.

Dental Care

Cavities are rare in dogs who eat normal canine diets free of sugary goodies, but gum disease is common, and your Dachshund's long, narrow muzzle makes him especially prone to oral problems. Food particles caught along the gum line harbor bacteria that form plaque. If plaque is not removed, it hardens into tartar (calculus), which irritates the gums and

causes gingivitis (inflammation of the gum). Allowed to progress, gingivitis can develop into periodontal disease, complete with abscesses, infections, and tooth and bone loss. Bacteria from an unhealthy mouth can spread throughout the body and damage the heart, liver, and kidneys. Fortunately, at-home dental care and regular veterinary attention will help to protect your Dachsie from gum disease.

How to Care for Your Dachshund's Teeth

Ideally, you should brush your Dachsie's teeth every day. Realistically, brushing two or three times a week will help to prevent tartar from forming and will alert you to broken teeth and other abnormalities. Use dental care products made for dogs; toothpaste for people can make your Dachsie sick, and doggy toothbrushes are smaller, softer, and different in shape from toothbrushes made for people. You might find a dental sponge (a small disposable sponge with a flexible handle) or a finger brush easier to manage than a regular

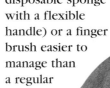

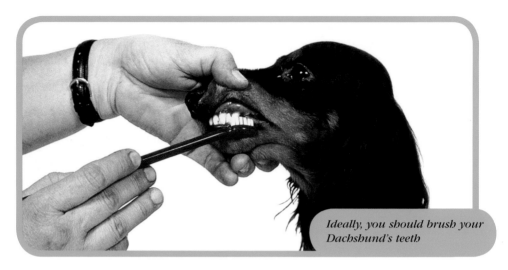

Ideally, you should brush your Dachshund's teeth

toothbrush. Ask your vet about canine dental products and their proper use.

Schedule dental checkups as part of your Dachsie's regular veterinary care. He also should have a thorough cleaning under anesthesia once or twice a year, depending on his individual needs. If your dog develops bad breath, visible tartar, bleeding gums, or other oral problems between regular examinations, schedule an exam. Early care can prevent bigger problems.

Feeding your Dachsie a high-quality dry dog food will help to keep his teeth and gums healthy. Appropriate chew toys and dental devices, or raw or sterilized beef bones, also can help.

If you have a Dachsie puppy, check his mouth and teeth every few days. Puppies are born without teeth and get their deciduous, or baby, teeth at about four weeks of age. The baby teeth are normally replaced by permanent teeth when your puppy is between three

and five months old, but sometimes a baby tooth is *retained* when the permanent tooth doesn't push it out completely. Retained deciduous teeth, most often incisors or upper canines ("fangs"), can push the permanent teeth out of alignment and keep the jaw bones from developing properly, leading to pain, difficulty eating, and other problems. If you think that your Dachsie puppy has retained a baby tooth, see your vet.

Anal Sac Care

Ever wonder exactly what dogs are smelling when they politely sniff each others' rears? Like other predators, every dog has a distinctive odor produced by anal sacs (anal glands) located on both sides and slightly below the anus. Healthy anal glands express, or empty, their fluid with every bowel movement. That's why dogs find poop so interesting—each pile says "I was here." Like any communication system, though, the anal glands don't always work properly. If they fail to empty themselves and too much fluid is retained, the glands can become impacted, creating discomfort. The dog may bite at his rear end or scoot along the ground, damaging the delicate tissue around his anus. Impacted anal glands also can make bowel movements difficult or painful and can develop into infections or abscesses.

How to Care for Your Dachshund's Anal Sacs

Impacted anal glands can often be relieved by squeezing out, or expressing, the fluid. The smell isn't as appealing to people as it is to dogs, but if you're brave you can have your vet or groomer teach you to express your dog's glands if necessary. Or you can just pay them to do it. If your dog's anal glands get impacted frequently, a high-fiber diet may help by creating bulkier stools that empty the glands when they pass. In severe cases, the anal glands can be removed.

Keeping your Dachsie well groomed is well worth the little bit of effort required. Your dog will be healthier and happier, not to mention oh so dapper! That can't help but make you a satisfied Dachsie owner.

49

Good grooming is essential for good health.

Chapter 5

Feeling Good

Your Dachshund will live longer and stay healthier
if you provide a healthful environment and learn
to recognize early signs of trouble. You are, after
all, his best friend and his first line of defense.
Your main backup is a good veterinarian.

Finding the Right Veterinarian

A good veterinarian is invaluable. You will entrust your Dachsie's health—in fact, his life—to your vet, and you will pay her significant money over the years, so don't settle for mediocrity. Your vet should show a genuine interest in your dog and should be willing and able to clearly answer your questions and discuss options. You should trust your vet, and your vet should respect you and your dog.

To find a good veterinarian, ask other dog owners, your obedience instructor, local dog clubs, breeders, and rescuers which vets they like and whether there is anyone they would avoid and why.

Annual Examinations

Your Dachsie should have a complete examination at least once a year—more often if he is a puppy or elderly, or if he has a chronic problem. Your vet will check your dog's overall condition, compare his current status to previous records, and note any changes. She'll listen to your Dachsie's heart and lungs, and check his back and joints. She'll examine his skin and coat, ears, teeth, gums, bite, and external eye area. If heartworm disease is present where you live or travel with your dog, your vet will check your dog for heartworm. She also will want a fecal sample to check for intestinal parasites. Your vet may recommend additional tests as well, depending on her current findings and your Dachsie's age and health history. Report anything odd about your dog's condition or behavior to your vet.

Vaccinations

A puppy born to a healthy, properly vaccinated mother receives disease-fighting antibodies in colostrum, a substance produced by the breasts for a few days after birth. This early protection wears off sometime between the fifth and tenth weeks. Unfortunately, this is also the age at which most puppies go to new homes, increasing their risk if exposed to disease. To rebuild immunity, puppy vaccinations are usually given in a

Talk to your vet about which vaccinations are right for your Dachshund.

series beginning between 5 and 12 weeks of age. Keep your baby Dachsie away from places frequented by strange dogs until he's fully vaccinated.

The Vaccination Debate

The best way to vaccinate dogs is a matter of much debate among veterinarians, researchers, and dog owners. Vaccination is necessary, but there is evidence that overvaccination weakens the immune system, leading to chronic health problems. Some vets and breeders still follow traditional vaccination protocols, which call for puppy vaccinations beginning at five to six weeks of age, followed by annual booster vaccinations. Others believe that puppy vaccines are effective for the life of the dog or that boosters should be given only every few years. Still others check the dog's immunity levels by testing for antibodies before vaccinating. How should you decide which approach is best for your dog? Learn what you can about vaccination, and ask your vet what she recommends. If you're uncomfortable with one vet's philosophy, find another vet.

Most canine vaccines are injected under the skin (subcutaneously) or into the muscle (intramuscularly). A few are given in nasal sprays.

Diseases to Vaccinate Against

Dogs are typically vaccinated against some or all of the following

diseases. (A number of other canine diseases, including Lyme disease and coronavirus, occur in some areas. Speak with your veterinarian about your dog's risk of exposure to these diseases or other diseases where you live or travel.)

Canine Bordetellosis

Canine bordetellosis, also called "kennel cough," is a bacterial disease of the respiratory tract. Although the cough itself sounds terrible, kennel cough isn't usually serious in an otherwise healthy adult. For a puppy, elderly dog, or sick dog, though, it can be fatal.

Canine Distemper

Canine distemper is a lethal, highly contagious viral disease. It causes respiratory problems, vomiting, and diarrhea and may affect the nervous

Should You Neuter Your Dachsie?

Responsible dog ownership includes a commitment to the lifelong welfare of any puppies your pet produces. You can relieve yourself of that responsibility and benefit your Dachsie's health by having your pet neutered. *Spaying* (removal of the ovaries and uterus) prevents pregnancy, cancers of the uterus and ovaries, and the constant hormonal shifts and twice-yearly heat cycles that make owning an unspayed female a challenge. *Castrating* (removal of the testicles) prevents testicular cancer, lowers the risk of prostate problems, and minimizes annoying stud-dog behaviors, including territorial urine marking, roaming in search of females in heat, and obsessive whining, pacing, slobbering, howling, and fasting when he finds one. An added benefit is that neutered dogs live longer. Neutering won't make your dog a wimp, and it won't make your dog fat unless you feed him or her too much.

system. Most puppies and about half of adult dogs who contract distemper die. Survivors are often partially or completely paralyzed, and they often lose some or all of their vision, hearing, and sense of smell.

Canine Leptospirosis

Canine leptospirosis is a potentially fatal bacterial disease of the kidneys that causes vomiting, vision problems, convulsions, and sometimes kidney failure. "Lepto" is spread in the urine of infected animals, including rodents. The disease appears in several strains but is rare in most areas. Many vets and owners do not routinely vaccinate against lepto because the risk of exposure is low for most dogs, and serious reactions to the vaccine are relatively common.

Canine Parainfluenza

The canine parainfluenza virus infects the respiratory tract, causing flu-like symptoms.

Canine Parvovirus

The highly contagious canine parvovirus (CPV), or "parvo," attacks the intestinal tract, heart muscle, and white blood cells, causing vomiting, severe and foul-smelling diarrhea, depression, high fever, and loss of appetite. Puppies who contract parvo often die within a few days, and those who survive may suffer permanent heart damage. The parvo virus is passed in the feces of infected dogs; is easily transported from place to place on shoes, paws, and clothing; and is extremely difficult to eradicate once it gets into an environment.

Infectious Canine Hepatitis

Infectious canine hepatitis is caused by a virus that attacks the liver and other tissues and may be fatal. It is spread in the urine of affected dogs. In mild cases, the dog may become lethargic or depressed and may stop eating. In more critical cases, symptoms may include sudden severe illness, diarrhea, and vomit that contains blood. The whites of the dog's eyes may turn yellow with jaundice.

Rabies

The rabies virus attacks the central nervous system of warm-blooded animals, and once symptoms appear, it is always fatal. Rabies is widespread in North America and some other parts of the world and can be passed to domestic animals. Most states require that dogs and cats be vaccinated against rabies, annually in some states and every three years in others. Your Dachsie should have his first rabies vaccination when he's about four months old and receive boosters as required by law.

Parasites

A parasite depends on another living thing, the host, to live. Some parasites are relatively benign, but some threaten your Dachshund's health and even his life.

External Parasites

Cartoons and humorous songs aside, fleas and other little critters are no laughing matter. They not only make your Dachsie uncomfortable, but they carry diseases that affect people as well as dogs.

Fleas

Fleas are tiny, hard-shelled, bloodsucking insects. They lay their eggs in grass, carpets, rugs, or bedding or sometimes on the host animal. The eggs and larvae can survive long periods without a host—in vacant buildings, for example. Fleas spread disease and tapeworm larvae and will bite people as well as pets. Many dogs are allergic to flea saliva, which causes them to scratch themselves raw, often leading to secondary infections.

If you find fleas on your Dachsie or in your house or yard, ask your vet about safe and effective flea control. You will need to treat all your pets, your home and yard, and possibly your car. Many over-the-counter flea controls are ineffective, and some products are dangerous

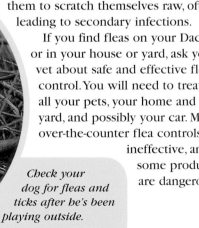

Check your dog for fleas and ticks after he's been playing outside.

55

in combination or even alone, so it's important to have professional guidance.

Mites

Tiny mites that eat skin debris, hair follicles, and tissue cause skin disorders referred to as mange. Some types of mange are contagious. Although the symptoms of different types of mange vary, they generally include hair loss, crusty, irritated skin, and severe itching. Animals with mange often scratch themselves raw, opening the way for infections.

Ringworm

Ringworm is a fungus (not a worm) that causes bald, often raw-looking patches. Like many fungal infections, ringworm is extremely hard to cure. It's also highly contagious and can infect people. Proper diagnosis is essential to effective treatment of ringworm, and home remedies are ineffective and may cause more problems. If your dog develops a sore or bald spot, see your vet as soon as possible.

Ticks

Like fleas, ticks are another common group of bloodsuckers. They are not insects but arthropods (relatives of spiders and mites). They are usually round and flat, although if they're swollen with blood or eggs, they look like beans with eight legs. Ticks carry diseases that attack dogs and people. The tiny deer tick, common in some areas, spreads Lyme disease, which can cripple its victim.

How to Remove a Tick

If you find a tick attached to your Dachsie, dab it with alcohol, iodine, or a strong saline solution to make it loosen its grip. Then, pull it straight out slowly with a tick remover, tweezers, or your fingers and a tissue. Don't squeeze—you may force disease-filled fluid into your dog. Clean the bite site with alcohol or antibacterial cleanser, dry, and apply antibacterial ointment. Wash your hands and the tick-removal tool. Call your vet if the bite becomes inflamed.

Ticks lurk in tall grasses, brush, and wooded areas for potential hosts to pass by, and they may be carried into your own yard and home. Check your Dachsie after he's been out— ticks don't usually attach to their hosts for a while after hitching a ride, and you may be able to remove them before they bite. If you find ticks on a regular basis, ask your vet about an effective prevention program, and inquire about the need for Lyme disease prevention where you live.

Internal Parasites

Nothing is quite as disgusting to most people as the idea of internal parasites. Unfortunately, worms and other parasites are among the most common organisms in our world, and those that affect dogs are easily spread from one animal to another. Although some parasites do little damage, others cause serious health problems and can lead to premature death. Fortunately, most common internal parasites are relatively easy to eliminate with regular veterinary care.

Heartworms

Heartworm disease is caused by a parasitic worm that invades the host animal's heart. As the worms reproduce, they fill the heart and blood vessels, causing congestive heart failure. Treatment for heartworm infection is expensive and hard on the dog, so prevention is the best cure. Heartworm larvae are carried from infected dogs to new victims by mosquitoes, and even if your dog spends most of his time indoors and rarely sees other dogs, he may become infected. If heartworm disease occurs where you live or travel with your Dachshund, use a prescription heartworm preventative. Because no medication is 100 percent effective, your Dachsie should be tested for heartworms every year or two.

Hookworms and Whipworms

Hookworms and whipworms are microscopic parasites that can be identified only with a microscopic examination of an infected animal's feces. Early infestations may go unnoticed, but once the worms mature and increase in number, they cause weight loss, bloody diarrhea, and anemia.

Roundworms

Roundworms look like spaghetti noodles about 8 inches (20.3 cm) long. Many puppies are born with them because the larva can be passed from mother to offspring, even if the mother herself has no symptoms of roundworm infection. Roundworms

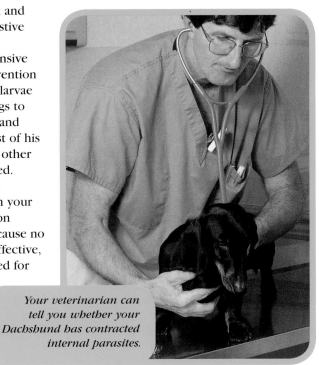

Your veterinarian can tell you whether your Dachshund has contracted internal parasites.

can cause nausea, vomiting, diarrhea
and anemia, and in high numbers
can cause malnutrition. Fortunately,
roundworms are easy to diagnose
and treat.

Tapeworms

Dogs get tapeworms primarily by
ingesting fleas that carry tapeworm
larva, although mice, rabbits, and other
animals are also possible sources. The
tapeworm requires an intermediate
host, and to acquire the parasite, a
dog must eat that intermediate host
while the worms are in the larval
form. The larvae then develop into
adult tapeworms in the new host.
Tapeworms don't threaten the health
of the host animal as severely as some
other intestinal parasites, but you
should still prevent them if possible
and eliminate them when present.

Health Issues in Dachshunds

Don't let this part of the book panic
you! Most Dachshunds are healthy, but
it is to your advantage to be aware of
health problems to which Dachshunds
are susceptible so that you'll know
what to look for if your dog becomes
ill and what special precautions you
can take to keep that from happening.

Bloat

Bloat, also known as gastric dilatation-
volvulus (GDV) or gastric torsion, is
a life-threatening condition that can
affect any dog at any age. Dogs with
deep chests, like the Dachshund, are
particularly at risk. Typically, a dog
bloats after eating food too quickly
and then exercising or drinking a large
amount of water.

Bloat occurs when gas forms in the
stomach, causing gastric distension

(that too-full feeling some people experience after holiday dinners). Sometimes belching or vomiting helps, but severe distension can cause the dog's stomach to twist, a condition called volvulus or torsion.

When torsion occurs, the esophagus is blocked and the dog can no longer vomit or belch. Pressure builds. The flow of blood into and out of the heart decreases, and heartbeat may become erratic. The stomach lining begins to die, and toxins build up. The liver, pancreas, spleen, and bowel may be damaged, and the stomach may rupture. The dog goes into shock. Death may occur quickly but not before the dog suffers considerable pain.

Symptoms of bloat or impending bloat include abdominal distention, retching, salivation, restlessness, refusal to lie down, depression, loss of appetite, lethargy, weakness, or rapid heart rate. If you suspect that your Dachsie is bloating, do not wait to see if he gets better. Call your vet or emergency veterinary clinic, and tell them you're on your way with a bloating dog. Drive carefully.

If your vet diagnoses bloat, she will treat your dog with intravenous fluids and steroids for shock, medication to control the erratic heartbeat, and antibiotics to fight secondary infections. She may try to insert a stomach tube to relieve pressure, and if this is successful, she will probably perform a gastric lavage to clean out the stomach. Or she may insert a large-bore needle directly into the stomach to release pressure. She also may

SENIOR DOG TIP

Living With a Senior Dachsie

Individuals age differently, but you can expect to see age-related changes when your Dachsie is between seven and ten years old. He may slow down a bit, become stiff in his movements, and take on a bony feel as he loses weight and muscle mass. He may not like changes in his routine or environment, and he may lose some of his hearing and vision. Most older dogs sleep longer and more deeply than when they were young, and some suffer from separation anxiety.

Your senior Dachsie continues to need regular exercise, grooming, and attention. Periodic checkups are essential for older dogs, and any sudden or extreme change in your Dachsie's physical condition or behavior warrants a trip to the vet. There's something very special about old dogs, so enjoy your Dachsie's golden years and help him do the same.

Feeling Good

suggest blood tests, X-rays, and an ECG.

Surgery to untwist the stomach and remove damaged tissue is often necessary. A dog who has bloated once is much more prone to bloat in the future, so some form of gastropexy may be done to anchor the stomach to prevent it from twisting. This surgery is sometimes used to prevent bloat if a dog has experienced gastric distension more than once or if he has close relatives who have suffered bloat.

If your dog survives, your vet may want to hospitalize him for a week or longer, and she will probably prescribe a special diet and medications when he goes home. Bloat is an expensive proposition for the owner, and sadly, even with treatment, many dogs who bloat die. Obviously, prevention is important.

As mentioned in Chapter 3, your Dachshund should eat two or three meals a day, not just one. Don't let him gulp down his food or exercise within two hours after a meal. If he eats quickly, scatter his kibble on the floor so that he has to pick it up a bit at a time, or purchase a toy that dispenses food as he rolls it. You also can slow him down by putting several rocks in his food bowl. (Make sure that they're too big for him to swallow.)

Orthopedic Problems

The "wiener" trait—the long spine carried on short legs—makes the Dachshund highly susceptible to spinal problems.

Canine Intervertebral Disk Disease

Disks are essentially cushions between the vertebrae. The spinal cord, that bundle of nerves that runs though the vertebrae, is covered by protective membranes called the meninges. When a disk herniates, or ruptures, it spreads

The Dachshund's long back makes him susceptible to intervertebral disk disease.

into the spinal canal, compressing the meningeal nerves, which then become inflamed.

Intervertebral disk disease is painful and often debilitating. The dog may lose control of his rear end and be unable to walk, and he may lose control of his bladder and/or bowel. Paralysis of the hind legs is also common.

Treatment for disk disease depends on its severity and other factors. If the damage seems minor, your vet may suggest crate rest to see if the injury will heal itself. Other options include surgery, hydrotherapy (swimming), physical therapy, chiropractic, acupuncture, drug therapy, and massage therapy. Some affected dogs can be helped to walk with support from a "rear-end harness" designed for that purpose or by placing a towel under the belly as a sling. Some dogs never regain the use of their hind ends, but if pain can be controlled, many of these dogs still live happy lives.

Many factors determine whether a particular Dachshund will develop disk disease. You have little or no control over some of them, but you can try to control others. If possible, discourage your Dachshund from jumping onto and off of furniture—either train him to stay off, or provide him with a ramp and teach him to use it. Don't allow people or bigger dogs to play roughly with your Dachsie. When you pick him up, support his rear end and body to keep his spine from overflexing. Teach children to pick him up correctly or not at all. Keep your Dachsie at a

FAMILY-FRIENDLY TIP

Kids and the Vet

Going to the vet can be scary, and not just for your dog! Fortunately, if you explain what's going to happen, a vet visit offers your child an opportunity to learn about responsible pet ownership and the importance of regular health care (for people as well as dogs). Before the visit, explain that regular checkups and vaccinations help to prevent sickness. Encourage your child to pet your dog while you wait to help to keep both of them more relaxed.

Vet visits also offer an opportunity to teach children how to be safe around pets. Tell your child that some pets are nervous when they visit the vet, and teach her never to touch any animal without receiving permission first from the owner.

Feeling Good

proper weight—a big fat belly is hard on a long spine.

Your Dachshund isn't fragile, but he's not as tough as he probably thinks he is, either. Of course, you can't eliminate all risks—sometimes a dog's gotta do what a dog's gotta do—but you can improve the odds that your Dachsie's back will stay healthy if you prevent him from jumping around,

Your Dachshund will be healthier if he receives a sufficient amount of exercise.

refrain from playing roughly with him, pick him up properly, and keep him at a proper weight.

Hip and Elbow Dysplasia

You may have heard of canine hip dysplasia and elbow dysplasia, which are serious problems in some breeds. Luckily, the incidence of these conditions is so low in Dachshunds that the Orthopedic Foundation for Animals (OFA), which screens and tracks inherited canine diseases, doesn't post overall numbers of affected Dachsies as it does for most breeds.

Metabolic Disorders

A metabolic disorder is caused when individual cells in an organ or gland malfunction. Some metabolic disorders are inherited, some are caused by environmental factors, and some require both a genetic predisposition and an environmental "trigger." Dachshunds are potentially subject to several metabolic disorders.

Cushing's Disease

Cushing's disease (hyperadrenocorticism) occurs in some Dachshunds and is caused by an oversupply of the hormone cortisol in the body. Common symptoms are excessive water consumption, and logically, excessive urination. Treatments include medications or surgery.

Canine Diabetes Mellitus

Canine diabetes mellitus (DM) occurs in Dachshunds, especially those who are allowed to become overweight. Symptoms include weight gain or loss, and excessive thirst and urination. If untreated, diabetes can cause seizures and shock, and it increases the risk of some other health problems. Diabetes can be treated with diet and various drugs, including insulin.

Hypothyroidism

Hypothyroidism is caused by a lack of sufficient thyroid hormone and can damage a dog both physically and emotionally. Symptoms may include hair loss, obesity or weight gain, lethargy, inflamed ears, or itchy, inflamed, crusty, scaly, or abnormally cool skin. Diagnosis can be difficult and is best accomplished with a complete thyroid panel. A simple thyroid test is often performed instead, but the results are not reliable. Treatment with a hormone supplement, most often L-thyroxine, usually effective.

Epilepsy

Epilepsy is characterized by seizures. If your Dachsie has a seizure, though, don't jump to a diagnosis of epilepsy. They can be caused by toxic chemicals, drugs, heatstroke, head injuries, or disease. When no clear cause can be identified, the dog is diagnosed as having primary or idiopathic epilepsy, which is considered to be inherited. If your Dachshund has a seizure, work with your vet to try to determine whether something in your dog's environment or history may have caused it. If so, it may be possible to remove the source of the seizures.

If your Dachsie has a seizure, stay calm. Keep your hands away from his mouth—he has no muscular control, and he could bite you without meaning to. If he loses control of his bladder and/or bowel, wait until the

seizure is over before you clean up. Keep your dog quiet, and call your vet.

Seizures are terrifying to watch but are rarely fatal. However, if they occur frequently, they can lead to hyperthermia (overheating), hypoglycemia (low blood sugar), exhaustion, brain damage, and even death. Primary epilepsy cannot be cured, but it often can be controlled with medication.

Eye Problems

Any Dachshund used for breeding should be examined annually by a board-certified veterinary ophthalmologist, and dogs with close relatives affected by inherited eye disease should not be used for breeding.

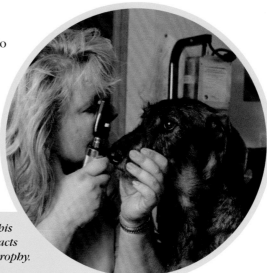

Certain eye problems affect this breed, including hereditary cataracts and progressive retinal atrophy.

Hereditary Cataracts

Dachshunds are susceptible to hereditary cataracts, which are opaque growths over the lens of the eye, causing partial or complete blindness in young dogs. (Not all cataracts are inherited—they also can be caused by injury, illness, and aging.) The only effective treatment is surgical removal.

Progressive Retinal Atrophy

Progressive retinal atrophy (PRA) is an inherited eye disease that affects Dachshunds and other breeds. PRA causes the retina (the light-receptive part of the eye) to deteriorate, resulting in partial or complete blindness. There is no treatment for PRA.

The Expert Knows

Pet Insurance

Several companies offer canine health insurance. Coverage and cost vary widely, as does customer satisfaction, so before you buy insurance for your Dachsie, ask your veterinarian and your dog-owning friends for feedback on their satisfaction with coverage from different companies.

Other Canine Health Problems

Some health problems can affect any kind of dog, including Dachshunds. Here are some of the most common.

Cancer

Cancers are among the most commonly reported life-threatening diseases in dogs. Most cancers strike in the second half of life, but some occur in younger dogs. The prognosis for a Dachsie with cancer depends on the type of cancer, the age and previous health status of the dog, how early the disease is detected, and other factors. Treatment options for dogs are essentially the same as for people—surgery, chemotherapy, and radiation therapy.

Your Dachsie's risk for some cancers can be eliminated or reduced. Removing the reproductive organs eliminates or lowers the risk for certain cancers. Reducing your Dachsie's exposure to various chemicals used around the house and yard, tobacco smoke, and other carcinogens also can reduce the risk of cancer.

Skin Problems

Skin problems, which can have a variety of causes, are not uncommon in dogs. Parasites and fungi account for some skin conditions, allergies for others. Sometimes the cause remains a mystery, and finding an effective treatment may require time and patience. Forewarned is forearmed, though, so let's take a look at some of the most common canine skin problems.

Eczema

Eczema is a term used for many skin disorders caused by various agents, known or unknown. Stress, food or drug allergies, sunburn, chemicals, and other things can cause eczema symptoms, which include itching, hair loss, and open sores. To diagnose a nonspecific skin problem and treat it effectively, you will need to work closely with your vet, keeping her informed of potential causes to which your dog may be exposed.

Hot Spots

Hot spots are inflamed areas of skin that often become open sores as the dog scratches and bites to relieve the itching. Many hot spots are caused by an allergic reaction to something in the environment—flea saliva is a common trigger, as are certain ingredients in dog foods, chemicals used in the house and yard, medications, and shampoos and other coat products.

Mange

Mange is caused by any of several species of tiny mites (relatives of ticks) that eat skin debris, hair follicles, and tissue. Dogs with mange typically suffer hair loss, crusty patches of irritated skin, and severe itching that prompts them to scratch themselves raw, providing easy entry for viral, fungal, or parasitic infections. Some types of mange are contagious; others are not. If you think your dog might have

mange, don't try home remedies—they probably won't work, and they may cause additional irritation and damage. Your veterinarian should take a skin scraping and examine it under a microscope to determine whether mites are present, and if they are, to identify the species that is attacking your dog. She then can prescribe an appropriate treatment program and tell you how to keep other pets safe from infection.

Emergencies

In any medical emergency, provide first aid, then get your Dachsie to a veterinarian as quickly as possible. Call ahead so that they know you're on your way, and drive carefully.

Common canine emergencies include the following:

Cuts, Bites, and Bleeding

Cuts, bites, and bleeding are not unusual in active dogs. If the wound is minor, clean it with clear water, and apply pressure with a clean towel or gauze pad to stop bleeding. Apply a topical antibiotic ointment, and watch the wound for a few days for signs of infection. If it continues to bleed or is deep or long, apply pressure and get your dog to your vet. If your dog is bitten by another animal, clean the wound, stop the bleeding, and call your vet. Bite wounds introduce bacteria from the mouth and may introduce disease, including rabies. Even if the wound doesn't require veterinary care, your vet will probably prescribe an oral antibiotic.

Fractures

Fractures (broken bones) are not uncommon in dogs. If you think that your Dachsie has a fracture, don't try to apply a splint—you could cause more damage. Keep your dog quiet, carry him (preferably on a blanket or board) to a vehicle, and get him to a vet.

Heatstroke

Heatstroke (hyperthermia) occurs when an animal's body temperature rises beyond a safe range. Symptoms include red or pale gums; bright red tongue; sticky, thick saliva; rapid panting; and vomiting and/or diarrhea. The dog may act dizzy or weak, and he may go into shock. Heatstroke can kill your dog or

cause serious, permanent injury, so if you suspect this medical emergency, wrap him in a cool, wet towel or blanket and get him to a vet. Just a few minutes in a closed vehicle on a warm day can be lethal!

Poisoning

Poisoning can be caused by many things: medications, chocolate, raisins, grapes, some plants, fertilizers, herbicides, insecticides, slug bait, rodent poisons, lead, antifreeze, insects, spiders, and snakes, to name just a few. Symptoms may include vomiting, diarrhea, loss of appetite, swelling, excessive salivation, staggering, seizures, or collapse. If you think that your dog has been poisoned, call your veterinarian, emergency clinic, or animal poison center immediately.

Alternative Therapies

Alternative, complementary, or holistic medical practices are based

Supervise your dog when outdoors in warm weather to prevent him from getting heatstroke.

on the belief that health is affected by emotional and physical factors. Alternative approaches to veterinary care include such formal disciplines as acupuncture, chiropractic, herbal therapy, and homeopathy. Some practices and practitioners are safe and useful, but some are not, so if you want to try alternative veterinary care for your dog, be cautious.

Acupuncture

Acupuncture in modern veterinary medicine involves the use of needles, massage, heat, and lasers to stimulate the release of hormones, endorphins, and other chemical substances that enable the body to fight off pain and disease.

Chiropractic

Chiropractic is based on the belief that proper alignment of the skeletal system, particularly the spine, is critical to the functioning of the nervous system and overall good health. If you decide to try chiropractic treatment with your Dachsie, find a licensed veterinarian who is also trained in chiropractic. A practitioner who lacks proper training in canine anatomy and physiology can cause serious injury to your Dachshund's vulnerable spine.

Herbal Therapy

Herbal therapy involves the use of herbs to treat disease and promote good health. Herbal therapy can be highly effective, but herbs should be used with great caution and only under the supervision of someone who is

knowledgeable about their properties. Don't confuse "natural" with "safe"— some herbs are extremely poisonous, and some that are useful in small doses can be lethal in larger amounts.

Homeopathy

Homeopathy is based on the notion that "like treats like," and homeopathic remedies are generally minute doses of substances that, in larger doses, would cause symptoms like those of the disease. As with other nontraditional forms of treatment, if you are interested in using homeopathy with your Dachshund, be sure that the practitioner is qualified to work with dogs, preferably with a degree in veterinary science.

Good health care is worth its weight in Dachsies to both you and your dog. Work with your vet and provide your Dachshund with proper nutrition and exercise, and he should be part of your life for many years.

Chapter 6

Being Good

Your Dachshund's actions are based almost entirely
on learning and inherited instincts. The only
exceptions, in fact, are abnormal behaviors caused
by illness, injury, or chemicals that affect his brain.
You can't change his instincts, but you can help
him learn to make the most of them with training.

What Is Dog Training, Anyway?

Training is the process of teaching new habits. Training goes on all the time, not just during your formal class or practice sessions. Your Dachsie is always learning, and if he repeats a behavior two or three times, it will probably become a habit. And as most of us know, it's easier to form habits than to change them once they're formed. Likewise, it's easier to replace a bad habit with a good one than to simply quit the bad habit.

Your Dachsie's forebears were bred to hunt, and modern Dachshunds retain the toughness and determination required for that job. Those traits can make Dachshunds challenging to train—they want to know what's in it for them. You need to teach your dog that learning is fun and rewarding, and that you are fair and trustworthy. You need to help your dog to be right, and the most fair and effective way to do that is through positive reinforcement, a process that rewards the dog for doing something correctly.

Consistency makes training much easier. If everyone in your household uses different words and training methods, or requires or allows different behaviors, your Dachsie will be confused. If you all use the same methods to teach the same things, he'll learn quickly. Consistency also means that you teach and reinforce your dog for good behavior all his life. An eight-week obedience class is a good start, but no dog is fully trained after a magical number of weeks of doggy school. If you help your Dachsie be a lifelong learner, you'll have a well-behaved, confident partner for many years.

Training Tools

You don't need a lot of equipment for basic obedience training, but the right equipment will make training easier for you and your Dachsie.

Collar and Leash

A collar and leash are essential. Tags can interfere with the effectivness of the leash, so you may want to have an extra collar on hand just to use for training.

Most experienced trainers prefer leather leashes because they are strong and flexible. For training your Dachsie, you will probably want a 4- to 6-foot-long (1.2- to 1.8-m-long) leash ¼ to ½ inch (0.6 to 1.3 cm) wide.

Have a favorite toy on hand to reward your Dachsie for learning.

Treats and Toys

You also will need some fun toys to reward your Dachsie for learning, as well as training treats. Training treats should be something your dog really likes: cooked meat, tiny bits of raw veggies, cheese, cereal, fruit (no grapes or raisins—they're toxic to dogs), commercial or homemade dog treats, or even bits of kibble from his daily ration. Keep them tiny, because treats add calories, and your dog shouldn't have to stop to chew. Also, don't hand out treats willy-nilly—have your Dachsie do something to earn each one.

Socialization

Socialization is an essential part of your Dachsie's education; it is the best way to counteract any inborn tendency toward shyness your dog may have. Socialization is especially important when your Dachsie is between 7 and 16 weeks old, a critical period during which puppies develop many social skills and attitudes. But socialization remains important throughout puberty and young adulthood.

How to Socialize Your Dachsie

To be properly socialized, your Dachsie needs to meet all kinds of people— male, female, young, old, different races, bearded, and clean shaven. He also needs to meet friendly dogs and other animals, and to experience all sorts of sights and sounds. Such experience will make him more confident throughout his life.

The Expert Knows

How to Talk "Dog"

Your tone of voice and body language are training tools. Dogs like happy voices, so be cheerful. Dogs also watch posture and movement, so stand up straight, relax, and be confident when you train. You and your Dachsie will both feel better!

If you have a young puppy, don't make the common mistake of postponing the start of his socialization. Although you need protect him from potential exposure to contagious disease if he hasn't completed his puppy vaccinations, you still need to make an effort to introduce him to friendly people, and if possible, animals before he reaches four months of age. So while walking him in a public park is not a good idea, carrying him in public places and letting people pet him is essential to his social development.

Crate Training

You can't watch your dog all the time as he learns to be trustworthy. When you cannot, a crate, used correctly, will keep your Dachsie and your belongings safe. Most dogs accept their crates as safe, comfortable, quiet "dens." Don't use a crate for punishment—it should be a refuge, not a jail.

Crate training will help to keep your dog and your belongings safe.

Your Dachsie's crate should be large enough for him to stand, turn around, and lie down comfortably. If you have a small, young puppy, use a smaller crate, or partition an adult-sized crate to limit the usable space. A healthy dog won't potty where he sleeps, so a smaller space will speed up housetraining. (Of course, if you don't want him to eliminate in the crate, don't line it with newspaper or wee-wee pads.) If your Dachsie likes to rip things up, don't give him any bedding, and be careful about the toys you leave in the crate— you don't want him to swallow the stuffing or squeaker from a toy.

How to Crate Train Your Dachsie

To teach your Dachsie to enter his crate willingly, toss a toy or treat in and say "Crate" or "Kennel." Give him a chew toy to keep him busy—make it something special that he gets only when in his crate. There's nothing like food to make a house a home, so feed your dog in his crate at first. If possible, put your Dachsie's crate in your bedroom at night. Remember, he's a pack animal, and you're his pack. He will feel isolated and lonely sleeping away from you.

If your Dachsie is not used to being in a crate, he may whine or bark at first. Don't let him out while he's raising a ruckus (unless you think he needs

to potty). If you let him out when he cries, he will quickly learn that noise gets him what he wants. Wait until he quiets down, and when he does, reward him with praise and a treat while he's still in the crate. Don't make a fuss or reward him when you let him out—if you do, you are rewarding him for escaping from the crate. The point is to make being in the crate a good thing.

Housetraining

Dachshunds can be hard to housetrain. Your Dachsie isn't stupid, and pottying indoors is not his attempt to "get even" with you. He just may not see the point of going all the way outdoors for a little thing like pottying, especially if it's raining or cold out. And his tough, independent nature may make him willing to take a scolding, if you can even bear to scold a guy with big, soft eyes. But if you are patient and persistent, your Dachsie will eventually get the idea.

Whatever your Dachsie's age, the key to housetraining is supervision. Don't give him the run of the house—or even the family room—if he still needs guidance. If your Dachsie is a puppy, keep in mind that he doesn't have complete control of his bladder or bowels. Like a child, by the time he realizes he has to go, your puppy may not be able to wait any longer. It's your job to teach your Dachsie where he should potty and to prevent accidents.

Puppies have to potty fairly often, around the clock—another reason to crate your pup in the bedroom at night. Typically, puppies need to go during or after every meal, first thing in the morning, last thing at night, after sleeping, after or during active play, and occasionally at other times. Don't expect a puppy to walk to the door and out—carry him. A healthy older dog can usually last seven or eight hours, although he may also need to go after eating, sleeping, or playing hard. Remember, the more accidents you prevent, the less likely your Dachsie will form the habit of pottying in the house.

How to Housetrain Your Dachsie

To teach your Dachsie where you want him to go, take him there on lead. Then wait. If he doesn't go within 5 minutes, crate him for 10 to 15 minutes, then take him out again. Don't let him run around the house—he may potty when you aren't looking, and his training will suffer. When your dog goes where you want him to, praise him and reward him with a little treat or short playtime. If your Dachsie is young, wait a little while before you take him inside—he may not be finished.

If you are housetraining an adult Dachsie, the training procedures are the same, but your dog should have better control for longer periods of time. He also should be able to control himself long enough to walk out the door on his own steam.

Until your Dachsie is reliable, keep him in the room you're in, and watch

How Long Can Your Dachsie Go Before Going?

Every dog is different, but you can estimate how often your Dachsie will need to potty by his age:

Age	Potty Schedule
8–12 weeks	at least every hour
3–4 months	every 2–3 hours
4–6 months	every 3–4 hours
6 months and older	every 4–6 hours, depending on the dog, his diet, and how consistent his housetraining has been in the past

him closely. Turning in circles, sniffing the floor, or arching his back while walking are all potty signals. If you see him doing any of those things or standing at the door, take him out immediately. Help him be right.

If you have to be away from your Dachsie longer than his capacity to "hold it," consider hiring a reliable pet sitter or dog walker to exercise him during the day. It's neither realistic nor fair to ask your dog to wait beyond his ability or to lie in his own waste if he can't wait.

Housetraining Accidents

Most dogs have at least one accident while learning. *Never* yell or punish your dog for an accident, and *never*

rub his nose in it. That's abusive and doesn't teach your Dachsie what you want him to do. You just have to help him understand that he should do it outdoors.

If you goof and let your dog have an accident, stay calm. Take him out in case he hasn't finished, then clean up the mess. You must remove all trace of odor so that your Dachsie doesn't think "this is the place." Regular cleaners will not fool his sensitive nose, so use a product that neutralizes organic odors (available from pet supply stores and many vets). After you clean up, go find your Dachsie, look into his beautiful eyes, and promise to supervise him more carefully in the future to help him learn. And be patient—reliable training can take several months.

Regardless of his age, if your Dachsie doesn't seem to have normal control of his bladder and bowels, talk to your vet—urinary tract infections, parasites, and other medical conditions can cause lack of control.

Basic Obedience Lessons

You can teach your Dachsie many things, but these basic commands are a good place to start, and they will make him a more pleasant companion.

Sit

Sit is a useful command that gives you control of your dog for your convenience and his safety. It also gives him a positive alternative to behaviors you don't want, like jumping on you or spinning in circles while you try to put his leash on him.

Dachshunds can be hard to housetrain, but with a little patience and persistence, your dog will get the idea.

Tips for Housetraining Your Dachshund

Your Dachsie will housetrain more easily if you:

- feed high-quality food to promote better bowel control and smaller, more compact stools
- don't expect him to wait an unrealistic amount of time before pottying
- don't give him the run of the house until he's reliable
- feed and exercise him on a regular schedule
- feed him at least four hours before bedtime, and don't let him drink water within two hours of bedtime
- keep his potty area free of feces—he doesn't want to step in it any more than you do

How to Teach Sit

Start with your Dachsie on a leash. Hold a small treat in front of his nose, *slowly* raise it just enough to clear his head, move it slowly toward his tail, and say "Sit." As his head comes up, his rear end will go down (unless you lift the treat too high—then he'll probably jump for it). As soon as his fanny hits

the floor, praise him and give him the treat. If he stands up before he gets the treat, don't give it to him. Have him sit, then give him the treat while he's sitting. Space several sessions of three or four repetitions throughout the day. When he responds quickly, stop guiding him with the treat, but do reward him once he sits.

When your Dachsie sits promptly on command, slowly increase the length of time he has to stay sitting to get the treat. Eventually you can wean away the treat most of the time. Do praise him, though, and give him an occasional goody. Keep the game interesting for him.

Come

Teach your Dachsie to come when you call him. It's a lot more convenient to have a dog who comes running than one who blows you off. More importantly, a dog who comes when called will be safer than one who doesn't.

How to Teach Come

To begin training, start with your Dachsie on a leash. Say "Fido, come!" *one time* in a happy, playful voice. Do whatever you have to do to get him to come to you without repeating the command. Go the other way, squat down, and play with a toy. If he doesn't come, gently pull him to you with the leash. If he starts to come on his own, stop pulling. When he gets to you, reward him—talk happily, and give him a treat, a toy, or a belly rub. Then let him go play. He should learn that

75

if he comes when called, good things happen. Repeat two or three times, then quit for a while. Do this several times a day.

Sounds simple, doesn't it? But how many dogs do you know who come every time they are called? Probably not many. And that is because most people inadvertently teach their dogs to ignore them. Here are some ways to avoid doing that:

- Never punish your Dachsie for coming to you, and never call him to do something he dislikes. Wait a few minutes before you do the "bad thing" (like nail clipping or confinement). Otherwise, go get him for these activities rather than calling him.

- Always praise your dog for coming when you call.

- Use the same word every time— "come" and "here" are common. Don't confuse him with different commands each time.

- Call only once—if you say "Fido, come! Come, Fido! Fido! Come!" your Dachsie will learn that you don't mean it. If he doesn't obey, go back to training with the leash.

- If your Dachsie doesn't respond reliably yet, don't give him a command you can't enforce. If you're standing in the doorway barefoot and wearing a towel, you aren't in a good training position!

Finally, even when your Dachsie is pretty well trained to come, never, ever let him off his leash in an unenclosed area. A single failure to come when called can get him killed.

Down
Down, like *sit,* is a very useful command for both safety and convenience. A Dachshund who will lie down and stay where you tell him is safely out from underfoot. A dog

Reward your Dachshund with a treat for coming to you when asked.

Kids and Dog Training

Involving your children with your Dachsie's training will help him learn that the kids outrank him in the pack. It also will help your children understand your Dachsie better. But be realistic. Unless your child has grown up training dogs under a good mentor, she won't have the skills or the judgment needed to train your dog fairly and properly. She can help, but an adult must be responsible for your Dachsie's training.

who learns to lie down on command is also a dog who has learned to respect people as his benevolent bosses, and he is less likely to behave like a little monster who thinks he's in charge.

How to Teach Down

You can teach your dog to lie down from a *stand* or a *sit*. Hold a treat in front of his nose, and slowly move your hand down and toward him while telling him "Down." As his head follows the treat, he should lie down. As soon as he's down, praise him and give him the treat. When he responds quickly and reliably, say "Down," but don't move your hand toward him. Slowly increase

the length of time he has to stay down before getting the treat, and praise and reward him while he's down, not after he jumps up.

Down is a hard command for some dogs because it is a submissive position. You may find that your Dachsie lies down at home but doesn't want to at obedience class. Be patient. As he gains confidence and learns that the other dogs won't pick on him, he should be more willing to lie down, especially if you use really yummy treats.

Stay

The *stay* command tells your dog not to move from a place and position—*sit*, *stand*, *down*—until you say he may do so.

How to Teach Stay

Put your dog in position and tell him "Stay." If he moves, gently put him back in the place and position where he was. Repeat the command just once— he needs to remember what you told him to do. When he has stayed put for a few seconds, praise him and give him a treat. Then release him—teach him a word such as "free" or "okay" to tell him he's off the hook.

Start with very short *stays*—a few seconds—with you standing very close. Slowly increase the time until he will stay for five minutes. Then move a step or two away, have him stay for one minute, and slowly build up again to five minutes. When he does that, add another step or two, shorten the time, and build up again. Always shorten the

A leash-trained dog will not pull or lunge on the leash.

How to Teach Walk Nicely on a Leash

If you're training a puppy or a reasonably responsive adult dog, try the "no forward progress" approach first: When your dog pulls, stop and wait until he stops. He may not notice immediately that you're not moving, but when he looks to see what the holdup is, praise him and start walking. If he pulls again, stop. You may do a lot of stopping and starting at first, especially if your Dachsie is used to pulling you along. But if you're persistent, your dog will soon discover that pulling makes you stop and not pulling keeps you moving. When your dog walks without pulling for a reasonable distance, praise him and give him a small treat as a reward.

If the stop-and-go approach doesn't work, you may need a different collar or halter. In fact, if you can't seem to get your Dachsie to respond to your training efforts, enroll in a good obedience class (or another one if you've been through one already) so that a knowledgeable instructor can help you find the best equipment and method for gaining better control of your dog.

How to Find a Good Obedience Instructor

You can learn a lot about training from books, magazines, and the Internet, but nothing beats a good obedience class taught by a qualified instructor. Ask

time when you increase the distance, and don't increase time or distance too quickly—add one step at a time. If your dog moves up, fidgets, or whines before the time is up, stand a little closer until he's comfortable again with that distance for that length of time. This is a stressful thing for most dogs to learn, so be patient.

Practice in different environments so that your Dachsie learns to stay where you tell him in any situation. Keep him on lead if you are in an unfenced area.

Walk Nicely on a Leash

Your Dachshund should be able to go for a walk without pulling and lunging against his leash.

Can You Teach an Old Dog a New . . . Anything?

It's never too late for obedience training. Adult dogs are able to focus longer than puppies, and they usually enjoy the special attention they get during training. Some adult dogs who have never been trained have to "learn to learn," but once they do, most become eager students.

people and dogs. She also should be alert and aware of what's happening in her class, and should not have so many people and dogs in one class that she cannot give each one some individual attention. In addition, the instructor should be available to answer questions for at least a few minutes after the class is finished. If you don't like what you see, look elsewhere.

Training takes some time and effort, but if you use a positive approach, you will find it enjoyable and effective. Every dog deserves to be trained!

79

your veterinarian, breeder, and dog-owning friends for recommendations, or do an Internet search. Observe a class or two before you sign up.

The instructor should above all appear to like and understand dogs. Her own dog or dogs should be well behaved (with some allowance if she has a puppy), and it should be obvious that she and her dog share a bond of affection and respect. She should treat her students and their dogs with respect, and if someone in the class has trouble with a certain training exercise, she should provide effective help. She should appear to be adaptable, adjusting her approach to suit different

Being Good

Chapter 7

In the
Doghouse

Even the most angelic Dachsie can be devilish at times. Luckily, if you train your dog, plan ahead, and respond quickly and appropriately to misbehavior, you can prevent or eliminate most problems. Before we get to specific issues, ask yourself some general questions when behavior issues arise.

- Why is your Dachsie doing what he's doing? Is he responding to instinct or stimulation? Is he bored and full of energy? Has he learned that behaving badly gets him what he wants? Could he have a health problem?
- Are you communicating clearly with your dog, or are you confusing him and accidentally reinforcing behaviors you don't want?
- Are you giving your Dachsie an acceptable alternative to the behavior you don't want?
- Are you proactive, taking steps to prevent unwanted behaviors before they happen?

Now let's look at some common unwanted behaviors and what you can do about them.

Barking

Barking is a natural means of canine communication. Your Dachsie barks to say "hello," "back off," and "let's play." He barks to ask to be let in or out, to get your attention, and to tell you someone's at the door or walking down the sidewalk. Chances are you understand your dog most of the time, and you respond.

Reasonable barking is normal and acceptable, but excessive barking is a nuisance. It is hard to stop because it's self-rewarding for your dog. If you're willing to invest a little time and effort, though, you can probably curb your Dachsie's enthusiasm for the sound of his own voice.

Solution

The first step is to try to figure out why your dog is barking so much. Is he bored or lonely? Is he excited by things he sees and hears around your home? Finding the reason behind excessive barking may give you a fairly simple solution. For instance, if he barks every time a squirrel dashes across the front yard, maybe you can limit his access to the front window.

Sometimes problem barking is linked to other behavioral issues such as separation anxiety, territoriality, or fear. If that's the case, you need to work on the underlying cause before the barking will subside. Obedience

If your Dachsie has a problem behavior that doesn't respond to regular obedience training, consult a qualified canine behaviorist.

How to Find a Canine Behaviorist

If your Dachshund has problem behaviors that don't respond to regular obedience training, a qualified canine behaviorist may be able to help. Be careful whom you choose—anyone can claim to be a dog trainer or behaviorist. To find a qualified person, ask your veterinarian for a referral, or go to www.animalbehavior.org.

training and remedial socialization may help.

Dogs often bark when they perceive an "intruder." Simply introducing your Dachsie to the neighbors and teaching him that having people around is a good thing may help him understand that he doesn't need to warn you every time the Joneses are in their yard.

Too often we yell at the dog for barking but give him no reward for being quiet. Remember, your Dachsie wasn't born knowing what "Be quiet!" means, and saying it more loudly doesn't make it more meaningful. A better approach is to have your

dog do something else—sit or lie down—to distract him and give you control. Praise him when he's quiet, and reward him. (See Chapter 6.) Some people even teach their dogs to "speak" and then teach "quiet" as an alternative, rewarding both behaviors when the dog does them on command. Consistency is critical. Don't ignore your dog's barking one time and yell at him the next.

Is there a quick fix? Manufacturers of bark collars (actually "don't bark collars") would like you to think so. These collars are supposed to discourage barking with an automatic punishment: an electrical shock, a squirt of a disagreeable odor, or a high-pitched sound. But they work on the symptom, not the cause. If your Dachsie barks because he's bored, he'll find a new hobby, like digging or tearing things up. If he's anxious or afraid, a bark collar will make the problem worse. And honestly, these collars don't always work. I've seen dogs with burns on their necks from barking through electrical shocks. Prevention, control, exercise, and training are the best ways to turn down the volume.

Chewing

Most dogs love to chew, especially when they're young. During the teething period, beginning around four to five months, a puppy's gums are swollen and sore as his permanent teeth come in. Chewing relieves the discomfort. Some dogs stop most of their chewing once their teeth are in,

The Lost Dachshund

Few things are scarier than having your dog get lost. If it happens to you, a few simple steps will improve the chances that you'll get your Dachsie back safely.

- **Identify.** Attach a current name tag, registration tag, and rabies tag to your dog's collar. Consider a microchip or tattoo for permanent identification—collars can be lost or removed. Permanent ID also gives you proof of ownership.
- **Act.** The sooner you start looking, the better the chances that you'll find your dog.
- **Call** all shelters and veterinarians in your own and nearby areas, as well as your closest Dachshund rescue organization. Visit area shelters as often as possible—shelter staff could overlook your dog.
- **Advertise** in your local newspaper, and consider advertising in newspapers from neighboring towns as well. A lost or stolen dog can turn up a long way from home. Check the found ads, too.
- **Use the Internet** to post information about your dog to discussion lists and bulletin boards. Ask readers to forward the information to other appropriate lists. Post photos if possible.
- **Post flyers** around your neighborhood, on store bulletin boards, and wherever else you can stick a poster. Include a color photo of your dog, where and when he was lost, and your telephone number(s).
- **Ask for help.** Give copies of your flyer to neighbors and local businesses. Ask area schools for permission to hang your poster where students will see it.

but others enjoy recreational chewing throughout their lives. It's up to you to teach your Dachsie what he's permitted to chew and what's off limits.

Solution

As with so many other behavior problems, prevention is the best solution to problem chewing. First, be sure that your Dachsie has several chew toys that he likes. Dogs have individual preferences, so if he doesn't care for one chewy, try another kind. Then, remove the things you don't want chewed from your Dachshund's reach, or watch him at all times. Teach your dog that he may chew some things but not everything. If he picks up something he shouldn't have, take it from him gently and replace it with one of his toys. Don't yell or punish him. Help him learn the rules. And be smart about the toys you give him—how is he supposed to know the difference between an old discarded shoe and your brand-new ones?

If you are not sure that your Dachsie understands, don't leave him unsupervised where he can get to things he shouldn't have. When you can't watch him, confine him to his crate with a nice chew toy or natural bone. Be consistent and think ahead, and your Dachshund will soon understand what's allowed and what's not.

Digging

It should come as no surprise if your Dachshund likes to dig. After all, his ancestors were bred to go after quarry underground. But you probably don't have any badgers living in your yard, and a serious digger can turn a lovely yard into a cratered moonscape. Fortunately, you can discourage inappropriate digging and redirect your Dachsie to activities that are acceptable to both of you.

Solution

If your Dachsie loves to dig and you have the space, give him a "legal" area in which he can move the earth to his heart's content. An area with loose sand or sandy soil, or even a sandbox, is cleaner than dirt and easy for your dog to dig in and for you to smooth out afterward. You can set up a barrier to confine the mess, and with a little planning, you can incorporate the "dig" into the landscape. Bury a toy or treat to give your Dachsie "quarry," and encourage him to dig in. If you see him excavating a different part of the yard, tell him "Leave it" and take him to his legal spot. Don't leave him alone in the yard until you're confident that he won't dig where you don't want him to.

If your Dachsie still insists on digging where you'd rather he didn't, fill or cover the hole with rocks, a pot, or some other barrier. Wire fencing buried under the top layer of soil in a garden also will prevent digging in flower beds or under fences but will still allow plants to grow.

Be sure, too, that you don't inadvertently promote digging. Soil amendments such as bonemeal and blood meal, for instance, smell like animal parts (which they are), and your Dachsie may try to dig out the animal he thinks is down there.

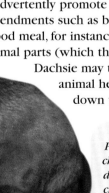

Prevent unwanted chewing by giving your dog an appropriate chew toy.

Several commercial products and home remedies are supposed to discourage diggers, but many of them don't work all that well and some are dangerous. Black and cayenne pepper sprinkled on top of the soil stop some but not all dogs. Mothballs are sometimes used to repel animals, but they are highly toxic. The biggest problem with all these products is that they offer no alternative behavior to use up the energy and drive that made your Dachsie dig in the first

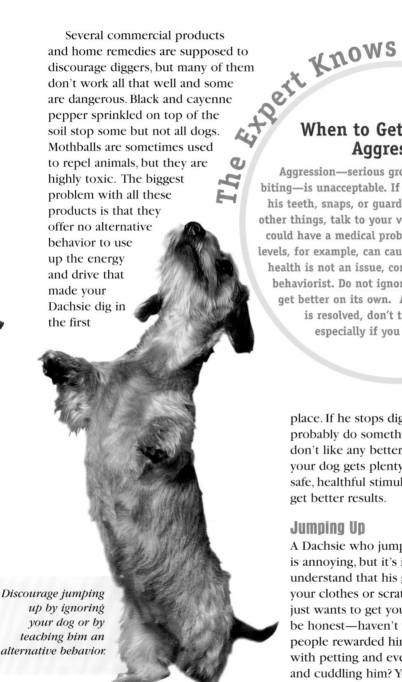

Discourage jumping up by ignoring your dog or by teaching him an alternative behavior.

The Expert Knows

When to Get Help With Aggression

Aggression—serious growling, guarding, and biting—is unacceptable. If your dog growls or bares his teeth, snaps, or guards his food, toys, bed, or other things, talk to your veterinarian. Your Dachsie could have a medical problem; abnormal hormone levels, for example, can cause aggressive behavior. If health is not an issue, consult a qualified animal behaviorist. Do not ignore aggression—it won't get better on its own. And until the problem is resolved, don't take any chances, especially if you have children.

place. If he stops digging, he will probably do something else that you don't like any better. Make sure that your dog gets plenty of exercise and safe, healthful stimulation, and you'll get better results.

Jumping Up

A Dachsie who jumps up on people is annoying, but it's important to understand that his goal isn't to dirty your clothes or scratch your legs. He just wants to get your attention. And be honest—haven't you and other people rewarded him sometimes with petting and even lifting him up and cuddling him? Your dog will stop jumping up only when he realizes that it won't get him what he wants. If you're consistent, he will learn. In fact, your family and friends may be harder to train than your Dachsie.

Solution

One approach is to ignore your dog when he jumps up. Simply cross your arms over your chest, turn your back on your dog, look up or away, and don't say a word. If he's used to getting a more interesting reaction, your Dachsie will keep trying for a while, but eventually he'll realize that jumping up makes you boring. When he gets off, praise him quietly and pet him. If he jumps up again, ignore him. To make this approach work, you must be patient and consistent. If you ignore your jumping dog one time but reward him the next by getting excited or petting him, he'll become even more persistent about pestering you.

Another way to discourage jumping is to give your dog an alternative. When you think that your Dachsie is about to jump up, tell him to do something else, like sit or lie down. When he does, reward him with something he likes—praise, cuddles, a treat, a romp in the yard. Of course, your Dachsie has to understand the alternative. If he doesn't know what "Sit" means, yelling "SIT! SIT! SIT!" as he paws at your shins won't teach him anything except that you're excitable and loud.

There are a few things you should *not* do to discourage jumping. Don't push your Dachsie away or down. Being pushed or petted rewards him

SENIOR DOG TIP

Older Dogs and Problem Behaviors

People often ask me if it's too late to train or retrain an older dog. Assuming that your dog is in reasonably good physical and mental health, it's never too late! (In fact, training should be a lifelong process of reinforcing what your dog already knows and learning new things from time to time.) An older dog with a long-standing behavior problem or general lack of training may require a bit more time and patience to train, but if you persist, you will succeed. Prevent unwanted behaviors with crate training, and take your dog to class if necessary. (If your Dachsie has developed aggression problems due to lack of training or other causes, be careful and ask your veterinarian where to get professional help.)

for jumping—he thinks that you are playing. Wait until he gets off on his own, then pet him. And *never* knee, kick, or hit your dog for jumping up. You could injure your dog and teach him not to trust you. No one is born knowing good manners, including your Dachshund, so it's up to you to teach him that politeness pays off and pushiness does not.

Nipping and Mouthing

If your Dachsie is still a puppy, he's probably mouthy. He played with his siblings and his mom by using his

Dachshunds

FAMILY-FRIENDLY TIP

Kids and Dog Problem Behaviors

If your Dachshund is exhibiting problem behaviors, be sure that a responsible adult supervises all interaction between your dog and children. If the problem is simply annoying, such as a housetraining lapse, the adult needs to control the dog's potty schedule and supervised freedom in the house. (See Chapter 6.) If the problem is potentially dangerous to your dog, such as bolting out the door or running away, be sure that your children can control the situation or confine your dog until an adult can supervise. If your dog displays aggressive behavior, confine your dog, teach your children to leave him alone, and get professional help immediately. Even a small dog can cause a serious bite—don't take chances with your children's safety.

mouth to bite, tug, grab, lick, and pull, so naturally he does the same with people. Some adults also use their mouths a bit too much if they haven't been taught not to.

Solution

One approach to prevent nipping and mouthing is to take away the payoff. Every time your Dachsie puts his mouth on you, get up, walk away, and ignore him for a minute or so, then return to what you were doing. If he pulls on your clothes or bites your ankles, leave the room for a minute and ignore him. Then come back and interact with him. If he doesn't grab you, he gets attention. If he uses his mouth, he gets ignored. Most dogs get the idea quickly.

Another approach is to give your pup something "legal" to munch on instead of flesh. If he mouths you, gently give him a toy in place of your hand.

Never hit your Dachsie for mouthing or nipping (or anything else, for that matter). Hitting doesn't teach your dog anything he needs to know and nearly always causes more problems than you had to start with.

If your Dachsie is a puppy, keep in mind that puppies are babies. When they get tired, they sometimes also get crabby or silly and do a lot more mouthing. If your puppy has been awake and active for a while and he's cranky or out of control, he may need a nap. Put him in his crate and let him sleep.

Potty Problems

Inappropriate elimination is a downright nasty problem behavior. Puppies, of course, have to be taught where to go. Older Dachsies sometimes have issues with housetraining for a number of reasons. If your dog was once reliable but is now pottying inside, have him checked by your vet before you begin retraining. Urinary tract infections, intestinal parasites, and other problems can rob your dog of control.

Solution

Once your Dachsie has a clean bill of health, you can proceed with training— or retraining. No matter how old your dog is, follow the housetraining procedures outlined in Chapter 6. Adhere to a regular schedule as much as possible, and never leave your dog loose in the house unsupervised until he's reliable. If you are on the couch watching television and your Dachsie pees in the bedroom, it's your fault, not his. For training to be most effective, every member of the household needs to understand and follow training procedures until your dog is reliable.

Remember, your Dachshund does not do naughty things to irritate you or get revenge. Most canine misbehaviors occur because the dog doesn't understand the human rules. You have to teach your dog. If you're as tenacious and forgiving as a Dachshund, you and your dog can solve most problems and strengthen your friendship at the same time.

Chapter 8

Stepping Out

Dachshunds enjoy being out and about, and many participate in various competitive sports and noncompetitive activities. Training, practicing, and performing are wonderful ways to channel your Dachsie's physical and mental energy, and to strengthen your relationship with your dog. Besides, they're fun!

Wherever You Go—Travel Tips

Dachshunds take their role as companions seriously, and most love to be with their people on the road as well as at home. Traveling with your Dachsie can be lots of fun, but please do a bit of advance preparation to make the experience safe and pleasant for both of you. Health threats to dogs vary from one place to another, so when traveling with your Dachsie, ask your vet about protection against any diseases or parasites that don't pose a threat at home.

Your Dachsie should always wear identification, but it's especially important when traveling. You can create temporary tags using write-in key tags, specifying where you will be during what dates. Include an alternate contact in case you become separated from your dog and you can't be reached. It's also a good idea to provide the name of someone who will take responsibility for your dog in the unlikely event that you are incapacitated by an accident.

Travel by Car

Many of us grew up with our dogs riding loose in our cars and hanging their heads out of the open windows. It seemed like a good idea at the time. But an unrestrained dog can be thrown around or out of the vehicle on turns and stops, and many dogs each year are injured or killed leaping or falling from car windows. Similarly dangerous is the practice of allowing a dog to ride on the ledge under the rear window. A quick stop could turn him into a flying missile, injuring the dog and anyone he hits. Your Dachsie may enjoy letting his ears fly in the wind, but dust and other debris hitting at the speed of a moving vehicle can seriously injure his eyes and ears. For the same reasons, dogs should never ride loose in truck beds.

Your Dachsie is much safer if he is restrained when riding in your vehicle. An airline-approved crate designed to withstand impact will protect your dog from injuries in an accident. It will also keep him from escaping if a door opens and will enable others to care for him if you are injured. A doggy seat belt is second best, although it won't protect him from impact. Seat belts should not be used where there are air bags—a deployed air bag can injure or kill your dog.

The heat in a parked car can kill your dog in just a few minutes even in relatively mild weather. If it's warm out, leave your Dachsie safe at home if he won't be able to get out of the car with you.

What to Pack for a Dachsie on the Move

- any medications your dog needs
- at least one toy (chewing is a good stress reliever)
- basic first-aid kit
- bowls
- brush and nail clippers
- food
- identification
- leash(es)
- water

Travel by Air

It's possible for your Dachsie to fly with you. If he fits into a carry-on pet carrier, he can join you in the cabin. If he's too large for that, he will have to fly as cargo and will need an airline-approved crate with food and water containers and absorbent bedding. Either way, he will need a health certificate signed by your vet within ten days prior to each leg of the trip. Carry a leash for preflight and postflight potty breaks.

Not all airlines transport animals, and those that do have individual policies that change from time to time, so check well in advance for booking requirements, prices, restrictions, and other details. If you're traveling abroad, be aware that some countries (and Hawaii) quarantine all incoming animals.

Competitive Activities

If you enjoy training your dog and like the thrill of competition, why not explore some dog sports? Dachshunds excel in earth events and tracking, and many do well in other sports. Win or lose, you'll form a strong bond with your Dachsie teammate, and that's better than a blue ribbon.

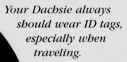

Your Dachsie always should wear ID tags, especially when traveling.

Agility

In agility, a dog negotiates a timed course of jumps, tunnels, and other obstacles under his handler's direction. Despite their short stature, many Dachshunds enjoy agility.

The American Kennel Club (AKC), United Kennel Club (UKC), and Australian Shepherd Club of America (ASCA) all offer agility programs, as do the United States Dog Agility Association (USDAA) and the North American Dog Agility Council (NADAC). The rules, procedures, obstacles, and jump heights differ from one organization to the next, so read the appropriate rule book before entering your dog in competition.

Conformation (Showing)

Conformation shows are designed to judge how well a dog conforms to the standard that has been established for his breed. To be successful in the conformation ring, your dog must come very close to meeting that standard. He cannot have any faults that are considered severe enough to disqualify him, and he cannot be altered (neutered). If you believe that your dog is of that high caliber, you may want to give it a try. You will need to learn how to groom and handle him properly for the show ring—presenting a dog properly is harder than it looks! Many kennel clubs and training schools offer instruction on show handling, and your dog's breeder or other people who show Dachshunds may be willing to teach you how to groom your dog for the show ring.

If you purchased your Dachsie from a responsible breeder, ask the breeder before you show your dog. If you bought him as a pet rather than a show prospect, you probably agreed to have your dog altered at a particular age, so that's one issue. Another is that serious breeders want only their best pups to be shown because any dog in the ring with the breeder's name on it reflects on the breeder's dogs and judgment.

Your dog may have a fault that has no affect at all on his quality as a pet but makes him unsuited for the show ring. Your breeder trusted you with her puppy, so return the favor by trusting her judgment.

The AKC and UKC offer conformation events.

Hunting Events

Although he's classified as a hound, the Dachshund also has some terrier-like traits—determination, toughness, and the instinct to follow prey into underground lairs. You may not want your dog dragging varmints home, but you can direct his instincts by training and competing in events designed to test his abilities above and below ground.

Go-to-Ground Trials

The American Working Terrier Association (AWTA) was established in

At a conformation event, a Dachshund is judged against the breed standard.

1971 to preserve the working instincts and abilities of terriers and to test those instincts and abilities through go-to-ground trials in which the dogs must demonstrate their hunting instinct by entering a natural burrow in pursuit of a prey animal. Dachshunds joined the list of eligible breeds in 1972. When the dog passes the Novice test, he progresses to the Open class, and a Certificate of Gameness is awarded to the dog who earns a perfect score of 100. The AWTA also offers a Working Certificate for dogs who go into natural burrows after quarry and either *draw* (drag out) or *bolt* (cause to run) the animal.

Earthdog Program

The AKC's earthdog program tests a dog's instinct and ability to follow prey through a "burrow," which may be a reinforced underground tunnel, or an above-ground construct of materials such as straw bales. Your Dachsie can earn earthdog titles at four levels. The "quarry," usually adult rats, are safely caged and often go right on munching their veggies while the dog barks like a fiend. Artificial quarry is sometimes used instead of live quarry.

Field Trials

Dachshunds also may participate in field trials, where their hound side takes over. AKC Dachshund field trials test the dog's ability to track game in hunting terrain and *give voice* or *bay* to let the hunter know where the animal is. The AWTA offers a Hunting Certificate for dogs who search for

What if My Dachsie Isn't Registered?

If your Dachshund is not registered but appears to be purebred and is altered, you can obtain an Indefinite Listing Privilege (ILP) certificate from the AKC so that your dog can participate in performance events. Some organizations (like the UKC, ASCA, and others) offer individual registrations for performance events to purebred and mixed-breed dogs. Contact the organizations for more information.

and locate quarry in actual hunts on a regular basis.

Obedience

Obedience trials, which are sanctioned by several organizations, test training and dog-and-handler teamwork. The term *obedience*, when used in the sense of competition, refers not just to the dog's willingness to obey a set of commands but the promptness and precision with which he does so. His handler's skill at guiding him through the exercises is also a factor in the team's final score.

The AKC offers obedience titles at all levels from Novice through the elite National Obedience Champion. The UKC and ASCA also offer obedience titling programs for which Dachsies are eligible.

Each obedience program has its own rules and requirements, but in general, your dog must earn three *legs*, or qualifying scores, in individual obedience trials, to earn a title. To earn a leg, he must score more than 50 percent on each exercise and at least 170 out of 200 possible total points.

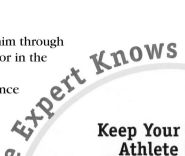

Keep Your Canine Athlete Safe

When introducing your Dachsie to a new activity, start modestly and progress slowly. Keep your dog at the proper weight and in good condition, warm him up before each performance, and be cautious about jumping or running him on hard surfaces. Don't ask your Dachsie to do anything for which he isn't properly trained. Keep in mind the special vulnerability of your Dachsie's spine, and be sure to handle him appropriately and to prevent him from engaging in especially risky behavior, such as leaping from too-high surfaces.

Rally Obedience

Rally obedience combines elements of competitive obedience and agility, requiring the handler and dog to negotiate a course of stations at which they demonstrate specific skills, including sit, down, stay, heeling, jumping, and so on. Rally is less formal and less stringent than obedience, and you may talk to your dog throughout the course and perform "do-overs" if you goof, which are not allowed in obedience. Competition and titles have been available from the Association of Pet Dog Trainers (APDT) since 2001. The AKC rally obedience program began in January 2005.

Tracking

Dachshunds are excellent tracking dogs, and tracking is a wonderful way to channel energy. It's also quite a thrill to watch your dog follow a track, or line of scent, that is completely outside your own sensory universe. You need to be able to follow your dog as he tracks across hill and dale, and the sport demands a lot of time for training, but you do not need much equipment. A harness and long line, flags to mark the track, small articles for your dog to find, a notebook and pen, food for rewarding your dog, and a good book on tracking are all the things you need.

Tracking tests evaluate your dog's

ability to recognize and follow human scent. Before you can enter an AKC tracking test, an AKC tracking judge must verify that your dog has passed a certification test. When your Dachsie successfully completes the Tracking Test, he earns the title Tracking Dog (TD) and becomes eligible for the Tracking Dog Excellent (TDX) or the Variable Surface Tracking (VST) tests. If he earns all three titles, he is a Champion Tracker (CT).

Noncompetitive Activities

One of the best things about living with dogs is that they keep us active. From a good old-fashioned amble around the block to therapy work, there's a noncompetitive activity for every dog and person.

Walking and Hiking

You and your Dachshund can both benefit physically and mentally from walking or hiking. You don't need a lot of equipment, but a few simple preliminaries will help to keep you both safe.

Make Sure That Your Dog Is Healthy

First, start slowly and build up over time. Schedule a veterinary checkup if it's been a while. Being out and about may expose your Dachsie to diseases and parasites, so be sure that his vaccinations are current. If you are traveling or hiking in wild areas, ask your vet whether your dog needs protection from organisms that don't pose a threat at home. Use heartworm preventive and an effective tick control as needed for the area, and be sure to have stool samples checked by your vet every few months.

Take care of your Dachsie's feet, and keep his nails trimmed short. (See Chapter 4.) Check for cuts or scrapes before, during, and after your outing, and for ticks, burrs, stickers, and other debris that may be caught on his skin or coat.

Dachshunds make excellent tracking dogs.

Check the Collar, Leash, and ID Tags

Check that your dog's collar fits and is in good condition, and that current identification, rabies, and license tags are securely attached. Use a leash—not only is it required by law in most places, but it can be the difference between life and death for your dog. A leash will also keep him from bothering other people, pets, and wildlife. A retractable leash is good

SENIOR DOG TIP

Traveling With Your Older Dachsie

If your older Dachsie seems confused, agitated, or nervous, or refuses to eat, drink, or eliminate normally when away from home, he may not enjoy traveling anymore. He'd probably be a lot happier at home. But if he seems happy and healthy, by all means take him along!

at times but can be a nuisance in the woods, and many parks require that leashes be 6 feet (1.8 m) or shorter.

Control Your Dachsie

Even a well-trained little Dachsie can be a handful if he picks up an interesting scent, and other animals occasionally pose a threat. Be sure that whoever walks your dog can control him and can respond appropriately to unusual situations. If your child wants to hold the leash, a responsible adult should supervise. What would your child do, for instance, if another dog attacked your Dachsie during a walk?

Watch the Weather

On hot days, keep walks short, avoid the hottest part of the day, and monitor your Dachsie's condition. It's a lot hotter where he is near the ground, especially on paved surfaces. Concrete and blacktop can become painfully hot and can reflect enough heat to raise your Dachsie's body temperature to dangerous levels.

Cold temperatures can be dangerous, too. Hypothermia (low body temperature) can be life threatening, and although frostbite is rare in dogs, it can occur, especially to the ears. Be sensible about the time your Dachsie spends outside in cold weather, and don't let him get chilled. A sweater or jacket may be a good idea.

In any season, try to keep your Dachsie off of areas where chemicals have been used. If you can't avoid them, wash your dog's feet with warm water and dog shampoo to remove toxic substances used on lawns or ice.

Provide Water

Be sure that your dog has frequent access to clean, cool water, especially in hot weather. If you plan to be out for long, or if it's hot, carry water with you. Collapsible pet bowls and all-in-one bottles and bowls are available from many pet supply stores, or you can teach your dog to drink from a squirt bottle. Try not to let him drink water from where you're hiking—it may be contaminated.

Pick Up After Your Dog

No one loves picking up poop, but leaving it for someone else to pick up—or step in—is downright antisocial. So stuff some plastic bags into your pocket, pick up after your dog, and dispose of the bags in a proper receptacle (at home, if necessary).

Your Dachshund may enjoy exploring the world through noncompetitive activities, such as hiking.

FAMILY-FRIENDLY TIP

Traveling With Kids and Dogs

Children and dogs can become excited while traveling, so take extra precautions to keep both safe on trips. An adult or older, responsible child should be the one to lift your Dachsie in and out of the car to prevent injuries or escapes. Teach everyone to check that your dog is either safe in his crate or fastened to a leash held by an adult before opening car doors, and to be sure that your dog is in a safe place before closing doors or hatches. Don't allow young children to walk your dog in new places—tragedy can happen in a heartbeat.

Many parks and natural areas prohibit dogs, so be sure that your Dachsie is welcome where you plan to go. If he is, obey the rules, pick up after him, and don't let him bother other people or animals. We are all responsible for making sure that dogs remain welcome.

The Dachsie Good Citizen

The AKC's Canine Good Citizen (CGC) program recognizes well-trained dogs and their responsible owners. The CGC test checks that your dog is well cared for, has basic training, is under control, and is polite around strange people and dogs. When your Dachsie has mastered the basics of polite behavior, you may want to test him.

Many dog clubs and other organizations offer CGC tests for nominal fees. You will need to show proof of rabies vaccination and provide your dog's own brush or comb. Your dog must wear a buckle or slip (choke) collar made of leather, fabric, or chain, and must be on-lead throughout the test. For more information, contact the AKC.

Calling Doctor Dachsie

If your Dachsie likes people, he might be a good therapy dog. Therapy dogs should not be confused with service dogs, those highly trained animals

Dachsies who like people might make good therapy dogs.

who assist people with special needs. Therapy dogs need good temperaments and solid obedience skills but do not need highly specialized training, and they do not have the legal rights of service dogs under the Americans with Disabilities Act (ADA).

Therapy dogs participate in two general types of activities: animal-assisted activities and animal-assisted therapy.

Animal-Assisted Activities

In animal-assisted activities (AAA), an animal and handler volunteer in nursing homes, literacy and reading programs, hospitals, schools, and other environments. No professional staff is directly involved with the visits, and no formal records are kept of the dog's effect on the people he visits.

Animal-Assisted Therapy

In animal-assisted therapy (AAT), the animal and handler work as volunteers with a professional therapist, teacher, or doctor who directs their activities and evaluates the effects on patients or clients.

Whatever activities you pursue with your Dachsie, please remember that you loved dogs before you loved the dog sports. Titles or not, as long as you and your dog love and respect one another, you win.

Resources

Associations and Organizations

Breed Clubs

American Kennel Club (AKC)
5580 Centerview Drive
Raleigh, NC 27606
Telephone: (919) 233-9767
Fax: (919) 233-3627
E-mail: info@akc.org
www.akc.org

Canadian Kennel Club (CKC)
89 Skyway Avenue, Suite 100
Etobicoke, Ontario M9W 6R4
Telephone: (416) 675-5511
Fax: (416) 675-6506
E-mail: information@ckc.ca
www.ckc.ca

Federation Cynologique Internationale (FCI)
Secretariat General de la FCI
Place Albert 1er, 13
B – 6530 Thuin
Belqique
www.fci.be

The Kennel Club
1 Clarges Street
London
W1J 8AB
Telephone: 0870 606 6750
Fax: 0207 518 1058
www.the-kennel-club.org.uk

United Kennel Club (UKC)
100 E. Kilgore Road
Kalamazoo, MI 49002-5584
Telephone: (269) 343-9020
Fax: (269) 343-7037
E-mail: pbickell@ukcdogs.com
www.ukcdogs.com

Pet Sitters

National Association of Professional Pet Sitters
15000 Commerce Parkway, Suite C
Mt. Laurel, New Jersey 08054
Telephone: (856) 439-0324
Fax: (856) 439-0525
E-mail: napps@ahint.com
www.petsitters.org

Pet Sitters International
201 East King Street
King, NC 27021-9161
Telephone: (336) 983-9222
Fax: (336) 983-5266
E-mail: info@petsit.com
www.petsit.com

Rescue Organizations and Animal Welfare Groups

American Humane Association (AHA)
63 Inverness Drive East
Englewood, CO 80112
Telephone: (303) 792-9900
Fax: 792-5333
www.americanhumane.org

American Society for the Prevention of Cruelty to Animals (ASPCA)
424 E. 92nd Street
New York, NY 10128-6804
Telephone: (212) 876-7700
www.aspca.org

Royal Society for the Prevention of Cruelty to Animals (RSPCA)
Telephone: 0870 3335 999
Fax: 0870 7530 284
www.rspca.org.uk

The Humane Society of the United States (HSUS)
2100 L Street, NW
Washington DC 20037
Telephone: (202) 452-1100
www.hsus.org

Sports

Canine Freestyle Federation, Inc.
Secretary: Brandy Clymire
E-Mail: secretary@canine-freestyle.org
www.canine-freestyle.org

International Agility Link (IAL)
Global Administrator: Steve Drinkwater
E-mail: yunde@powerup.au
www.agilityclick.com/~ial

North American Dog Agility Council
11522 South Hwy 3
Cataldo, ID 83810
www.nadac.com

North American Flyball Association
www.flyball.org
1400 West Devon Avenue #512
Chicago, IL 6066
800-318-6312

United States Dog Agility Association
P.O. Box 850955
Richardson, TX 75085-0955
Telephone: (972) 487-2200
www.usdaa.com

World Canine Freestyle Organization
P.O. Box 350122
Brooklyn, NY 11235-2525
Telephone: (718) 332-8336
www.worldcaninefreestyle.org

Therapy

Delta Society
875 124th Ave NE, Suite 101
Bellevue, WA 98005
Telephone: (425) 226-7357
Fax: (425) 235-1076
E-mail: info@deltasociety.org
www.deltasociety.org

Therapy Dogs Incorporated
PO Box 5868
Cheyenne, WY 82003
Telephone: (877) 843-7364
E-mail: therdog@sisna.com
www.therapydogs.com

Therapy Dogs International (TDI)
88 Bartley Road
Flanders, NJ 07836
Telephone: (973) 252-9800
Fax: (973) 252-7171
E-mail: tdi@gti.net
www.tdi-dog.org

Training

Association of Pet Dog Trainers (APDT)
150 Executive Center Drive Box 35
Greenville, SC 29615
Telephone: (800) PET-DOGS
Fax: (864) 331-0767
E-mail: information@apdt.com
www.apdt.com

National Association of Dog Obedience Instructors (NADOI)
PMB 369
729 Grapevine Hwy.
Hurst, TX 76054-2085
www.nadoi.org

Veterinary and Health Resources

Academy of Veterinary Homeopathy (AVH)
P.O. Box 9280
Wilmington, DE 19809
Telephone: (866) 652-1590
Fax: (866) 652-1590
E-mail: office@TheAVH.org
www.theavh.org

American Academy of Veterinary Acupuncture (AAVA)
100 Roscommon Drive, Suite 320
Middletown, CT 06457
Telephone: (860) 635-6300
Fax: (860) 635-6400
E-mail: office@aava.org
www.aava.org

American Animal Hospital Association (AAHA)
P.O. Box 150899
Denver, CO 80215-0899
Telephone: (303) 986-2800
Fax: (303) 986-1700
E-mail: info@aahanet.org
www.aahanet.org/index.cfm

American College of Veterinary Internal Medicine (ACVIM)
1997 Wadsworth Blvd., Suite A
Lakewood, CO 80214-5293
Telephone: (800) 245-9081
Fax: (303) 231-0880
Email: ACVIM@ACVIM.org
www.acvim.org

American College of Veterinary Ophthalmologists (ACVO)
P.O. Box 1311
Meridian, Idaho 83860
Telephone: (208) 466-7624
Fax: (208) 466-7693
E-mail: office@acvo.com
www.acvo.com

American Holistic Veterinary Medical Association (AHVMA)
2218 Old Emmorton Road
Bel Air, MD 21015
Telephone: (410) 569-0795
Fax: (410) 569-2346
E-mail: office@ahvma.org
www.ahvma.org

American Veterinary Medical Association (AVMA)
1931 North Meacham Road – Suite 100
Schaumburg, IL 60173
Telephone: (847) 925-8070
Fax: (847) 925-1329
E-mail: avmainfo@avma.org
www.avma.org

ASPCA Animal Poison Control Center
1717 South Philo Road, Suite 36
Urbana, IL 61802
Telephone: (888) 426-4435
www.aspca.org

British Veterinary Association (BVA)
7 Mansfield Street
London
W1G 9NQ
Telephone: 020 7636 6541
Fax: 020 7436 2970
E-mail: bvahq@bva.co.uk
www.bva.co.uk

Canine Eye Registration Foundation (CERF)
VMDB/CERF
1248 Lynn Hall
625 Harrison St.
Purdue University
West Lafayette, IN 47907-2026
Telephone: (765) 494-8179
E-mail: CERF@vmbd.org
www.vmdb.org

Orthopedic Foundation for Animals (OFA)
2300 NE Nifong Blvd
Columbus, Missouri 65201-3856
Telephone: (573) 442-0418
Fax: (573) 875-5073
Email: ofa@offa.org
www.offa.org

Publications

Books

Anderson, Teoti. *The Super Simple Guide to Housetraining.* Neptune City: TFH Publications, 2004.

Boneham, Sheila Webster, Ph.D. *The Complete Idiot's Guide to Getting and Owning a Dog.* New York: Alpha Books, 2002.

Ewing, Su. *The Dachshund.* Neptune City: TFH Publications, 2005.

Morgan, Diane. *Good Dogkeeping.* Neptune City: TFH Publications, 2005.

Magazines

AKC *Family Dog*
American Kennel Club
260 Madison Avenue
New York, NY 10016
Telephone: (800) 490-5675
E-mail: familydog@akc.org
www.akc.org/pubs/familydog

AKC *Gazette*
American Kennel Club
260 Madison Avenue
New York, NY 10016
Telephone: (800) 533-7323
E-mail: gazette@akc.org
www.akc.org/pubs/gazette

Dog & Kennel
Pet Publishing, Inc.
7-L Dundas Circle
Greensboro, NC 27407
Telephone: (336) 292-4272
Fax: (336) 292-4272
E-mail: info@petpublishing.com
www.dogandkennel.com

Dog Fancy
Subscription Department
P.O. Box 53264
Boulder, CO 80322-3264
Telephone: (800) 365-4421
E-mail: barkback@dogfancy.com
www.dogfancy.com

Dogs Monthly
Ascot House
High Street, Ascot,
Berkshire SL5 7JG
United Kingdom
Telephone: 0870 730 8433
Fax: 0870 730 8431
E-mail: admin@rtc-associates.freeserve.co.uk
www.corsini.co.uk/dogsmonthly

Websites
www.nylabone.com

Index

Note: Boldfaced numbers indicate illustrations; an italic *t* indicates tables.

Index

Dachshunds

About the Author

Sheila Webster Boneham, Ph.D., loves dogs and writing about dogs. Three of her books have won the prestigious Maxwell Award from the Dog Writers Association of America, including *The Simple Guide to Labrador Retrievers*, named Best Single Breed Book of 2002. For the past decade, Sheila has taught people about dogs through her writing and other activities. She hopes that her successes and mistakes as a puppy buyer, breeder, trainer, owner, and rescuer can benefit other dog lovers and their dogs. Sheila and her canine companions are active in competition and in dog-assisted activities and therapy. A former university writing teacher, Sheila also conducts writing workshops. You can visit Sheila and her dogs on the web at www.sheilaboneham.com.

Photo Credits